OPEN MY EYES

A Doctor's Powerful Story of Courage & Healing

OPEN MY EYES

A Doctor's Powerful Story of Courage & Healing

PETER LEE POWERS, M.D.

Copyrighted Material

Open My Eyes: A Doctor's Powerful Story of Courage & Healing

Copyright © 2025 by Peter Lee Powers. All rights reserved.

No part of this publication may be reproduced, stored in retrieval system or transmitted, in any form or by any means—electronic, mechanical, photocopying, recording or otherwise—without prior written permission from the publisher,
except for the inclusion of brief quotations in a review.

For information about this title, contact the publisher:

Peter Lee Powers
openmyeyespowers@gmail.com

ISBN-13: 979-8-218-56342-4 (softcover)
ISBN-13: 979-8-218-56343-1 (eBook)
Library of Congress Control Number: 2024925317

Printed in the United States of America

Cover photo: Peter Lee Powers, M.D.
Cover design: EagleLadyDesignStudio.com

Foreword

When I went blind in 1984, I was already fully trained as a family doctor and was board certified by the American Board of Family Medicine. I was thirty-four years old and had already been working in my own medical practice for four years.

I recovered my sight in 1985. My struggle involved several surgeries and lots of heartbreak. About that time, friends and acquaintances who had heard about my journey with type 1 diabetes and recovering from blindness started telling me I should write a book.

I would probably have never even started this book without the persistent encouragement and prodding of two very close friends who were brothers, Kris and Kevin Cassidy. They had both done some writing previously, and they agreed to work with me to get my story down on paper. I acknowledge and credit them for all their help in the early stages of the writing while I was living in Alaska.

When I left Alaska and moved to Prescott, Arizona in 1991, I started a new life and a new medical practice. The book writing project ended up on a shelf in the garage.

After I finally retired from the practice of medicine in 2020, two months before I turned seventy years old, I thought about picking up the book project again. It took three more years of retirement and encouragement from those who'd read the manuscript before I actually made the commitment to bring it back to life. One of my friends from church, Colleen Eagle, a recently retired professional medical editor, agreed to work with me to complete this book. Without her assistance, this book would still be on a shelf in the garage, unfinished and unpublished.

I wrote the book primarily to encourage people with health and life challenges to never give up on themselves, and to never lose hope in their most difficult times. There is always something that can be done to make things better. There is always a place for and benefit in holding positive expectations. There is always help available in friends, family, or professional caregivers. There is always light at the end of a tunnel, even if we can't see it at the time.

I have experienced immense joy in my life. It is much more than simply the joy of overcoming hardship, and the joy of getting out of the darkness and into the light. I have the joy of so much gratitude for so many wonderful people in my life. I have experienced so much love all along the way. I have had so many special experiences with people. I have been so blessed in my role as a doctor and teacher who could help people when they needed it.

All of the times that I was also a patient made me a better physician. I have felt all the frustration of waiting in offices, not understanding what my choices were, and being fearful of the outcomes of surgery. Those experiences have made me more compassionate. I have felt fulfilled in striving to be the best "me" that I can be.

I celebrate that I continue to keep learning and growing. I have been a farm kid, a good student, an athlete, and a traveler to many foreign places. As a doctor, I have shared people's laughter and tasted their tears.

I have been a boyfriend, a husband, a stepdad, and a dear friend to many. I have been a hiker, a skier, a cyclist, a kayaker, a backpacker, and a marathon runner. I loved all these things. I loved being a motivational speaker. And now, I am loving being a writer.

I continue to work on myself to be a better man, a better human being, and the best possible version of myself. I never expected that picking up this book project would turn into such a "life review" while I was still alive, which supposedly happens after we pass away.

My life has been so worth it to learn what I have learned through experience. Because this book is largely focused on my healing journey during a specific challenging period, many other parts of my life and the people who were a part of it, are not included. That does not diminish their role in helping me to be the person I am today. For the friends who are included in the following pages, I have used first names only to protect their privacy.

Thank you to everyone I have ever met along the way.

Much love, Dr. Peter Lee Powers, January 2025

A toast to your courage,
A hug from your bear,
The love of your woman,
And a family that cares.

The love of your brothers,
The gift of your friends,
Parents who love you —
These loves never end.

Your touch is healing,
Your voice very clear,
You hear people's laughter,
You taste of our tears.

Your vision is greater
Than eyes ever see.
Let the gifts that you've given
Be the gift that you receive.

Written for Peter by his mother, Barbara Powers, on the day of his first eye surgery, June 12, 1984.

Contents

Chapter 1: My Life Was Interrupted 1

Needles and Oranges 3
Setting Expectations 5
No Guarantees 6
Bright Green Sweatsuit 8
Local Hero 9

Chapter 2: Owen Center Road 12

Passages 15
Look Homeward Angel 19
Seize the Day 20
The Miracle of Healing 21

Chapter 3: From Edinburgh to Boston 23

The Candy Bar Heresy 24
Squeeze Bottles 27
"Go, Farnland!" 29
A New Tradition 32
Pushing the "Envelope" 35

Chapter 4: Gross Anatomy 39

Give and Take 41
Running the Gauntlet 41
Trade-offs 44
On Call 45
The Miracle of Life 47
Drawing the Line 48
Residency 49
Making Allowances 52
The Healing Arts 53

Chapter 5: The Maroon Bells 55

Forever Young 57
Ashes to Ashes 58
Living in the Present 59
The Good Son 60

Chapter 6: The Black Flag 62

An Unhealthy Pace 63
The Need to Be Needed 67
A Helping Hand 69

Chapter 7: An Atmosphere of Celebration 71

Being a Patient 72
Breaking Down Roles — Peter, the Unhelpful 74
Challenging the System 76
Reaching Out 77

Chapter 8: Dancing Blind 79

"Blind" School 80
Improving My Signature 82
"Attitudes" Class 83
Obstacles and Opportunities 85
Being a Friend 87
Affirmations and Visualization 88
Resisting Isolation Through Dancing 91
A Victory of Sorts 92
Growing Confidence 95
Choosing Happiness 96

Chapter 9: Light 98

Quieting Doubt 100
Practicing Medicine 102
Navigation and Inspiration 105
Healing From Within, Help From Without 106
A Blind Physician 107

    A Kindred Spirit *109*
    Looking Good, Sounding Bad *111*

Chapter 10: Run River Run **113**
    Willing to Be Happier *116*
    Chariots of Fire *118*
    Another Tragedy *120*

Chapter 11: Searching for Meaning **124**
    "Australian 9 Day" *124*
    A Team Transformation *127*

Chapter 12: Watching the River Run **130**
    Four Women *136*
    A Leap of Faith *140*

Chapter 13: Ocean Kayaking **143**

Chapter 14: The Sunny Southwest **147**
    My New Family Practice in Prescott *148*

Chapter 15: A Picture of Health **150**

Chapter 16: My Sore Foot **155**

Chapter 17: What a Party! **161**
    RAGBRAI XXII — 1994 .... *162*
    Golf *168*
    Healing Self and Others *169*

Appendix: Factors in Healing **171**

1

My Life Was Interrupted

Rain, rain and sun! A rainbow in the sky!
A young man will be wiser by and by . . .
— Alfred Lord Tennyson, "Gareth and Lynette"

I discovered my illness in a tangle of moments between high school geometry and farm chores. I was a fourteen-year-old schoolboy living on our family farm ten miles outside Rockford, Illinois, trying to figure out how I fit in.

My father was a mechanical engineer who worked in a factory that made automatic assembly machines. On evenings and weekends, he farmed Christmas trees, along with wheat, corn, alfalfa, and soybeans, an enterprise he had undertaken to pay for our college educations. My mother had a doctorate in education and taught high school math and science.

Dad was what was known as a "sundown farmer," meaning that he had to work each day from sunup to sundown, so he called our farm "Sundown Farm."

I was the oldest boy, and shared responsibility with my older sister for looking after our two younger brothers and younger sister. We all put in a lot of time on evenings and weekends doing chores and working with my father.

On the farm I acquired the habit of doing whatever

We sold Christmas trees for $2.50 per tree at Sundown Farm.

needed to be done without having to be told. It was good training.

We worked hard, but there was also time to play, like riding our workhorse, Pegasus, and spending time on our 4-H projects. Our family also enjoyed holidays at our Weeona Lake cabin in Wisconsin.

I'd always set high standards for myself. For example, in 4-H club, which rewards hard work with success, I was named the county Grand Champion for my forestry projects for three consecutive years. I wasn't the greatest athlete, but I was wiry and strong for my size, and I was always willing to try.

At age 12, riding Pegasus

During my freshman year, I had short-lived success as a wrestler, winning my first official match against a more experienced varsity wrestler. The coaches were excited about my potential, and for about a week I enjoyed the promise of getting a varsity letter. My wrestling career ended with appendicitis on Thanksgiving Day, 1964.

My parents were slow to take action when I developed stomach pains after our big turkey dinner. I was writhing in pain from appendicitis, but was told, "Oh, you just ate too much," which was probably true, and was sent off to lie down to recover. The pain increased in intensity, and after several hours, they finally realized I needed to see the doctor. We were not at home on the farm, but spending the holiday at the Weeona Lake cabin, so we had to go to the local small-town hospital to get medical help.

The operation was uneventful, but the surgeon stated that with another hour's delay, he thought my appendix would have ruptured, a serious condition that might have taken weeks in the hospital to recover from, if I even survived it at all. As it turned out, I was able to go back to the cabin the next day. My lasting takeaway from the entire experience was, "What does it take to get anyone to listen to me?" I learned I had to pay attention to what my body was telling me and to trust my instincts.

During February 1965, I suddenly found that I was thirsty and hungry and tired all the time. Craving an energy boost, I would dip into the sugar bowl, but nothing seemed to pick me up. I found myself needing to urinate constantly, and I was losing weight. In this condition, I would miss a day of school, go a day, then miss a day. This went on for two weeks, and I didn't know what to make of it, but I knew something wasn't right because I had always been very healthy.

When I was finally taken to our family doctor, Dr. Joe Perez, a local general practitioner, he said I had the classic symptoms of diabetes. The diagnosis didn't mean anything to me. I just knew that I felt bad and was glad somebody knew what was wrong. When my mother heard the diagnosis, she cried. In 1965 most doctors still regarded diabetes as a slow walk to an early death, with stops along the way to suffer disability from a long list of possible complications.

Although the symptoms that characterize diabetes had been observed since antiquity, it wasn't until 1889 that researchers established the role of the pancreas in the disease. Insulin was discovered in 1921, and it was 1922 before treatment with insulin injections was introduced. Prior to 1922, most people died within about three weeks after being diagnosed with type 1 diabetes.

The doctor did a blood test to confirm his diagnosis. When he came to his outer office where I had been waiting to talk about the test results, he found me unconscious. He hospitalized me directly.

Needles and Oranges

It was during that two-week hospitalization that I got my first idea as to what diabetes might mean to my life. One morning, after I was starting to feel better, a stocky, red-haired nurse appeared at my bedside and announced that I would need to learn how to give myself insulin shots. I did not welcome the idea. The other nurses had been giving me my shots, and if I had to get shots, I wanted them from somebody who knew how to give them. But the red-haired nurse had an imposing presence that made arguing out of the question. She produced a syringe and orange and told me I was going to practice giving shots to the orange. The idea was that injecting the orange would be like injecting myself. She showed me how to hold the syringe between my thumb and first finger, like a dart, and poke it into the orange. I decided to placate her. Hopefully, I could just play around with the orange and needle until she went home and then go back to the old system. After she left, I learned from one of the other nurses that this was unlikely. I had been talking to the head nurse.

Throughout the day, I injected the orange with water until it was leaking and squirting water all over the place. I was having fun. The head nurse returned that evening and informed me that it was now time for me to try giving a real shot. To my surprise, she rolled up her sleeve and offered her own arm.

"Don't worry. It doesn't hurt," she insisted.

I just looked at her, still not believing that she wanted a shot from me.

"Go ahead," she prodded.

Watching her face for any sign of a flinch, I took the syringe between my thumb and first finger and poked the needle into her arm. She didn't flinch. Still watching her face, I slowly depressed the plunger, injecting the sterile water, which we were using in place of insulin. I was looking so closely for signs of pain that I was hardly even paying attention to what I was doing. She looked thoughtful, as if she might have been thinking about what to have for dinner. It was a good sign.

After I pulled the needle out, she announced that it was now time for me to give myself a shot. Encouraged by my apparent success, I filled a new needle and poked it into my own arm.

I was startled by how painful it was. Needles in those days were not microfine and not disposable. They were big, 22-gauge size. The syringe was glass, not plastic. I was also startled to find that the sterile water left a painful reservoir in my skin. It took several minutes after I'd pulled the needle out for the disorienting feeling of surprise and pain to wear off. After it did, it struck me that I'd just given myself a shot. It seemed impressive. I could do something most people couldn't do, something doctors and nurses did.

After the head nurse left, I thought about why the shot hurt me but hadn't seemed to have hurt her. Over the next few days, I practiced injecting oranges and myself. As I imitated the relaxed manner of the head nurse and worked on my technique, I found that the shots hurt less and less. Eventually they didn't hurt at all. Confidence seemed to be important.

Setting Expectations

The doctors at the hospital explained to me that people with diabetes had lost the ability to produce insulin, which is the hormone that helps the body to transfer sugar from the bloodstream into the cells where it is used for energy. They said that for the rest of my life I would be taking shots to get the insulin my body needed.

The doctors said that it would be important for me to stay in good "diabetic control," which meant that I needed to keep the amount of sugar in my blood within a certain range. Too much sugar in my blood would make me feel extreme fatigue and hunger like I had before my hospitalization. Too little sugar could cause a medical emergency called "insulin shock," which could kill me. To keep my blood sugar well-regulated, I would have to follow a diet—one that required me to eat regularly, measure out what I ate in exact amounts, and avoid sweets altogether.

The doctors also informed me that in about twenty years I could expect health complications—perhaps blindness, kidney failure, or nerve damage. The risk of these complications was less, I was told, if I stayed in good diabetic control.

While fear of blindness, kidney failure, and nerve damage convinced me that I wanted to be a "good diabetic," the kind who always follows his diet, it also ingrained in me the belief that serious complications were likely. One of the brochures the doctors gave me on diabetes had a drawing of a blind man holding a white cane and a beggar's cup. This might be me someday. The picture stuck in my mind.

A vague sort of uneasiness also stuck with me. I was too inexperienced to put my finger on it or understand what it was at the time. Later, I realized it was because I was playing a game where my life and health were at stake, but I had no way of knowing how I was doing.

I was supposed to keep my blood sugar within a certain range, but I had no way of knowing what my blood sugar level was. The only exact information I could get came from the blood test that the doctor gave me a couple times a year.

On a day-to-day basis, I had no way of knowing if my conscientious efforts to avoid eventual kidney, eye, and nerve damage were working. It would be fifteen years before home glucose monitoring would become available to people with diabetes.

No Guarantees

Because I was a good kid, respectful to adults and obedient, I was very accepting of my diabetes. I even told everybody about it when I returned to school, and my classmates and coaches were very supportive.

Up to this point, my diabetes had caused me little more than inconvenience. A few weeks later, events took a more threatening turn.

I was out pruning Christmas trees on our farm with my brothers and sisters. We had been working for quite a few hours without taking a meal break. I began to get tired and cranky, and I finally announced that

Pruning Christmas trees on the "back 40" at Sundown Farm

I didn't want to prune anymore. I continued to work, however, and I began to get disoriented. I had to ask my brother Stephen several times which tree I had been pruning.

Soon I had lost track not only of the tree but the row I was supposed to be working on. My brothers and sisters didn't understand what was happening and were impatient with me. Finally, I gave up trying to focus on the trees, and I just laid down in the field.

Realizing something was wrong, my oldest sister, Ellen, ran back to the house, which was about a half mile away, and got my parents. They drove out in the pickup truck and took me home. Recognizing that I needed sugar, they tried to give me marshmallows and orange juice with sugar in it, but I refused.

"I'm not supposed to have sugar," I insisted.

I was too delirious to understand what was going on. After some prodding, I drank the juice. It brought my blood sugar back up quickly. Within a few minutes I was back to normal physically, but frightened, wondering if I might have died.

The next day, when we went in to see Dr. Perez, he explained that my extreme fatigue and disorientation were symptoms of insulin shock, which results from an imbalance between insulin and blood sugar. My blood sugar had dropped well below normal as a result of both the strenuous work and my failure to eat. But my insulin dosage was also too high. He said he had been expecting this reaction because my blood sugar level had been decreasing every time he checked it. He had been planning to decrease my insulin dose accordingly.

I'd always had great faith in my doctor, who was well-respected by everyone, but I was taken off guard by his response. I felt upset.

I thought to myself, "Well, you can be casual about this because it didn't happen to you!" But I had been in real danger, and my family was frightened. I was too polite to ask the doctor out loud what was uppermost in my mind: If he knew it might happen, why didn't he warn us?

This experience shocked me into the awareness that I couldn't depend on others, even doctors, to be responsible for my health. I needed to know what was going on with my own diabetes. It also created a fear of being out of control and helpless. I realized that I could follow all the rules, I could do everything "right," and I still might not be safe.

If following the rules didn't guarantee safety, I wondered, what does? It was one of those questions I would spend a lifetime trying to figure out.

Bright Green Sweatsuit

In 1966, people with diabetes were generally discouraged by their physicians from engaging in sports or other vigorous exercise. Dr. Perez had the wisdom to recognize that good health required exercise and active involvement. He encouraged me to keep playing high school sports and living fully. This advice surprised a lot of people, but coming from a medical doctor it had the ring of authority.

A good friend, Mike, had been trying for some time to talk me into trying out for our school's cross-country running team. Mike had won a varsity letter, a highly coveted award, as a freshman. I decided to try cross-country running, partly at Mike's urging, but mostly because I wanted a varsity letter.

In our first time trial, I was surprised to find that I was one of the top seven runners on the team, which meant that in my very first race I was privileged to run in a varsity uniform. This uniform included a bright green sweatsuit, which carried a lot more status than the gray sweats the junior varsity wore. In that race I finished in the top third of the field, and I was excited when I learned that my time would help determine how our team did.

Things went smoothly until midway through one of the next races, when I noticed that I was starting to feel the same kind of aches and fatigue I had felt when I went into insulin shock in the Christmas tree field. I was frightened, and I slowed down as I ran the last mile. As I neared the finish, I began to feel delirious. I focused on getting to the finish line, where I found some food and immediately began to eat.

Initially, that experience was scary, but ultimately it gave me more confidence in being able to take care of such problems on my own. It also motivated me to find a way to keep my blood sugar from getting low during races. I was not about to give up running or my green varsity sweats.

I soon discovered that the key to successful workouts and races was to make sure that I had a snack just before running so that my blood sugar wouldn't get too low. Classmates would often kid me about how often I got to snack. I took their kidding as support, and I enjoyed it.

Although I had a healthy respect for the dangers of insulin shock, I had soon adopted my doctor's attitude toward diabetes and sports. I decided that I was going to do all these things in spite of my diabetes. I wasn't going to let it stop me.

"I may have diabetes, but I'm fast," I thought.

By the end of my sophomore year, I was the third fastest runner at Rockford's Boylan Central Catholic High School and had won the varsity letter I so much wanted.

Local Hero

During my junior and senior years, I was the fastest long-distance runner at my high school. Teachers and friends would often come to watch me run, and the support felt great. I was determined to prove that it didn't matter if I had diabetes. I could do anything anyone else could do. I made every effort never to use my diabetes as an excuse or make anyone else responsible for it. I wanted to be just like everyone else.

By my senior year I was closing in on the school two-mile record and was one of the top runners in our conference. A runner from a nearby school, John, had clocked a faster two-mile than I had and was the favorite to win the conference.

My high school senior photo, 1968

The top two finishers from the conference meet would get to compete in the state championships. I'd been getting a buildup for a trip to State all year from my coaches, teachers, and friends. Only one other runner from my high school had ever gone to State. He was a legend in my school. I had seen pictures of him and even met him once. His records still stood in both the one- and two-mile. I liked to think that I might be remembered with the same respect and awe as this runner.

The conference meet took place on a beautiful autumn day at Beyer's Stadium, a cinder track in Rockford. I was excited because my dad had come to watch me race for the very first time. I knew he was proud of me, but he worked long hours and hadn't ever taken time off to see me run in competition. I really wanted to please him. I wanted to win.

In the pre-race excitement, I felt nervous and a little upset. My blood sugar began to drop. Noticing my loss of energy, I began to eat apples—five Red Delicious apples—right before the race to try to get my blood sugar back up. By the time we lined up for the starting gun, I felt my energy level was back to normal.

As we started the race, John and I moved to the head of the field and began to put distance between ourselves and the remainder of the pack. As John and I vied back and forth, I thought I could feel the apples bouncing around in my stomach. But I knew I'd chewed them. At least they weren't bouncing around whole, I thought.

Going into the last lap, I decided to make a show of strength, and I passed John on the outside of the track. This was a risky strategy because it meant that I was actually having to run a slightly greater distance than John. I pulled two strides ahead with about 300 yards to go, then 200. Leading down the back stretch, I hoped to outrun him now. At 100 yards we both broke into an all-out sprint. With 50 yards to go he pulled up next to me. At 25 yards he edged past me. He crossed the finish line one step—two-tenths of a second— ahead of me.

My time of nine minutes fifty-nine seconds was a new two-mile record for my high school, and it qualified me to go to State. But as I collapsed into the arms of friends who were congratulating me on my finish, all I felt was intense disappointment at losing in front of my father. I was so caught up in my emotions that I never talked to him about how I felt.

It was a surprise to me many years later to hear my father say that he was proud of me that day. That was mostly what I wanted from the race. Today, what gives me the most pleasure about that day—more than setting the school record or earning a spot for my picture on the school trophy wall—is simply that my father saw me run.

Senior Peter Powers set a school record in two mile run with a blazing 9:59 in the District meet. Powers effort qualified him to run in the State meet on Saturday.

The irony is that years later when talking to my dad about the race, he remembered the event as if I *had* won.

At the 1968 Illinois State Championship meet there was a large field of talented runners. Some of the runners had posted times so much better than mine that I didn't look at the event as a chance to win. I was just glad to be able to participate. I ran better than expected. I ran twenty-five seconds faster than John, who had bested me by a step to win the conference a few weeks earlier. That day I placed 8th in the State of Illinois two-mile championship. The afterglow stuck with me for a long time. My diabetes hadn't kept me from being a part of things. I not only fit in, I was also a success.

2

Owen Center Road

> *To everything there is a season, and a time to every purpose under heaven: A time to be born, and a time to die; a time to weep, and a time to laugh; a time to mourn, and a time to dance.*
> —Ecclesiastes 3:1–4

In our family we thought of the two youngest children, Kenny and Charlotte, as being the "little kids." The "older kids"—my older sister Ellen, born in 1949, myself, born a year later, and my younger brother Stephen, born in 1951—competed among ourselves. But we all looked out for Kenny and Charlotte, and I was especially proud of their accomplishments the way a big brother sometimes is.

Kenny was a good athlete, and he made the cross-country team the year he was a freshman and I was a senior. I liked having him on the team with me and feeling that he looked up to me both as an older brother and as the fastest runner on the team.

Charlotte was the baby of the family, and she was poised and self-confident from all the love and attention she had received all her life. She was outgoing and popular with her classmates and was selected to be a cheerleader.

Clockwise from top: Mom, Ellen, me, Charlotte, Kenny, Stephen

Open My Eyes: A Doctor's Powerful Story of Courage & Healing

Clockwise, L to R: Dad, Stephen, Kenny, Mom, Charlotte

Charlotte was also very artistic, wrote poetry, and sang and played the guitar. When she was younger, we had a very informal family band. Ellen, Stephen, and Charlotte played guitar, and I played the drums. Charlotte had a beautiful voice, but she would not stick to the tempo I set. I told her several times that I was the drummer and that I set the tempo, but it never made any difference. Charlotte continued to play to her own rhythms.

Kenny and Charlotte were both competitors and confidants to one another. When the Boylan Central Catholic High School put on its annual play, Kenny was picked to be the student director, and Charlotte was selected as the female lead. The play was a big event at their school, and I enjoyed thinking of the excitement they would be feeling at being the center of so much attention. There was never any question that I was going to drive the two hours down from the University of Wisconsin at Madison, where I was going to school, to see them perform.

When I arrived home, I found my mother feeling excited about the play and pleased that I had come to see it. Kenny and Charlotte had already left the farm for the high school to get ready for the evening's performance. I spent some time catching up on family news with my mother and Mary, a family friend. Then we were interrupted by a phone call. It was the state police. Kenny and Charlotte had been in a head-on collision on Owen Center Road. Charlotte was dead. Kenny was seriously injured. The paramedics were still at the scene.

I went numb. Charlotte dead. Kenny hurt. The images screamed in my head. Panic twisted wiry and sharp inside me. Not dead. Please, not dead. Somehow, I felt there had to be a way to stop all this from happening. I began to be aware of a sensation that I could do anything—rip the metal away from the car frame with my bare hands to free Kenny and Charlotte if I had to, run with them in my arms to the hospital. I was prepared to do anything.

Mary, mother, and I rushed to the car. Mother said she couldn't drive so I did. I was barely aware that I was driving. When we got to the crash site, police squad cars lined the road. Their garish flashing lights isolated the area around the two mangled automobiles in faint puddles of red light. The paramedics had used the Jaws of Life to pry back a portion of the engine, which had smashed through the passenger compartment, trapping Kenny and crushing Charlotte against her seat. Her body had already been removed and sent to the morgue. Kenny was in an ambulance about to be taken to the hospital.

We had come too late to do anything. We followed a police car at high speed to the hospital. I raced intently as if that could help me regain position on the terrible reality that had overtaken us.

At the hospital everything came to a sudden suffocating halt. We were put in a small room for families just adjacent to the emergency room. There we could hear Kenny screaming as the doctors worked on him. He screamed things I had never heard from him before. Each scream seemed as if it were ripped from someplace deep inside him. "It's killing me! Jesus Christ, it's killing me! Help me! God dammit, help me! Please help me!"

I learned later that Kenny was unconscious at this time and that his screaming and swearing were typical of instances of serious head injury. Even if I had known that at the time, I am not sure it would have given me any comfort. Some part of his soul was being tortured, and I couldn't do anything for him. He was no longer trapped in wreckage that I could attempt to tear away to free him. I could no longer run for help or carry him to safety. I knew nothing about how to help treat him. I needed so much to be able to help, and I was so completely unable. Over and over, I searched the perimeter of that small room for some way to turn back the nightmare that had engulfed us, for some way to bring us all back safely to where we had been. I tried comforting my mother. There was nothing else I could do.

Our parish priest had come to the emergency room shortly after we had arrived. He tried to be reassuring. He told us that Charlotte was with God; that she was not hurting; that we shouldn't be upset because she was all right. He said that the doctors were doing everything that could be done for Kenny, that everything would be okay and that we needed to be quiet and rest and allow ourselves to accept the situation.

I resented the priest. I resented him for trying to comfort us when that was the only thing that I could still do. I resented him for being as powerless as I was. I promised myself then that I would never be that helpless again. I hadn't known until then what I was going to do with my life. Now I knew. I would become a doctor. If I were a doctor, I wouldn't be helpless in those situations. I could do something. Something.

The screaming seemed to go on for a long time.

Passages

In the days that followed, I replayed the accident in my mind hundreds, perhaps thousands, of times. If someone or something distracted me for a moment, the gnawing tightness in my stomach drew me immediately back to my task. I reviewed where I had been, what I had heard, what I had done. I put the pieces together, over and over. It didn't make any sense. Charlotte was so young, only fifteen, and so beautiful. Why Charlotte? God . . . why Charlotte?

I had never experienced this kind of loss. Nothing had prepared me for it. As farm kids, we had had lots of animals and pets. When our animals died, I felt sadness, but it was quickly crowded out by all the other living going on around me. The loss I had experienced with my diabetes seemed minor. I was so full of living and growing that my diabetes seemed to be merely an inconvenience. Nothing in my life had come close to the huge gaping hole left by Charlotte's death and my fear that Kenny, too, would die.

As I began to accept that Charlotte really was dead, I felt intense overwhelming sadness for all the things that I would never have with her again. I don't remember ever having been told while growing up that men should not cry, but at some level I knew the rule. Losing Charlotte shattered any impulse I had to respect the rule, to be strong or stoic. I cried for Charlotte.

My fear that Kenny might die balanced against my grief over Charlotte's death. He remained in intensive care in very critical condition. In addition to his head injuries, most of the major bone groups on the right side of his body had been broken. The doctors put him in traction and put a pin in the femur in his right leg. A plate was put in his right forearm to help several broken bones to heal. His jaw was wired shut to promote healing in a facial fracture.

Each new surgery increased the risk that Kenny might die of complications. After Kenny's jaw was wired shut, the doctors decided not to try to repair the bone damage to his right shoulder. They feared that he might be unable to clear his airway if complications caused him to vomit, and he might suffocate.

There wasn't anything I could do to help Kenny while he was in intensive care. I couldn't help with his medical treatment. I couldn't even feed him or wash him or read to him. I felt useless, helpless. So I did the only thing I knew how to do. I willed that he would live. Growing up as a Catholic, I knew that prayers were sometimes answered, but as a young person with diabetes, I had learned to rely on myself to stay healthy. I leaned on my willpower to heal Kenny.

The police had determined soon after the accident that the driver of the other vehicle had been driving under the influence of alcohol. The district attorney's office was planning to prosecute and ask for the most severe penalties. They planned to use the case as a rallying point to push for changes in the law to crack down on drunk driving. Looking back, I can see that this was their way of showing that they were not powerless in the face of such a tragedy. When the driver of the other vehicle died, the district attorney's office lost its defendant and its resolve to make changes in the law.

When I learned that the other driver had been intoxicated, I was stunned. I couldn't accept that such a senseless thing could happen. I hated him. It was only when he died that I realized that I had wanted him to live. He died from complications caused by the fracturing of some of his large bones. Almost all the large bones on the right side of Kenny's body were broken. The death of the other driver made me realize how serious Kenny's condition was. I became even more fearful that Kenny would die.

After the accident, our family opened our home to friends and relatives who wanted to come and express their grief and support. I remember feeling a sense of responsibility to be like my father, to keep my chin up and help other people get through this. Perhaps I adopted this attitude as part of the role I had assumed in the family as the oldest brother. I may also have used helping others as a way to avoid my own pain over Charlotte's death.

However, it was clear to me at the time that I was benefiting in a very direct way from being there for others. I loved hearing people say how wonderful they thought Charlotte was and how much they had loved her. I would think of all my own wonderful memories of her and feel tremendous love for her. When I felt that love, I didn't feel the pain in the same way anymore. People would also say how much they respected our family and how wonderful it was that we were opening our home during this time of grieving. All this love and support filled me with a sense of being valuable, of being safe and secure.

The tragedy of the accident had touched people well beyond our own family and friends. There were a number of articles in local and national newspapers along with a great deal of community concern. A funeral service and Mass were held three days after Charlotte's death at the Catholic church, and mourners filled the building and spilled out into the street. Another service was held at the high school, which filled the gymnasium. At that service members of our family talked about Charlotte and what a wonderful person she was. We shared poetry she had written, and we sang with the congregation.

An artist's portrait of Charlotte Powers, who died in a car crash at age fifteen in 1969

I think it is unusual for a family to receive as much community support and as many opportunities to grieve as we did. Perhaps because of this, my grieving over Charlotte's death began to turn into a celebration of her life and a realization of what a wonderful gift it was to have shared in her life.

The burial procession stretched for miles from the cemetery down a road near our house. At the gravesite we again sang and shared memories of Charlotte and our love for her. I felt so much a part of the whole community when we sang, that in those moments I really didn't feel the sadness anymore. After Charlotte's coffin was lowered into the grave and the ceremony completed, everyone left except for some family members and a few friends.

Someone suggested that my brother Stephen and I fill in the grave. In tears, we shoveled dirt over Charlotte's casket, and I accepted for the first time in a really complete way that she was gone from this life. I felt much more peaceful after that. I realized that there would still be changes I would have to make and lessons to learn and pain to go through, but I understood that Charlotte was gone, and that it was time for me to go on living and to go about the business of helping Kenny heal.

Look Homeward Angel

Kenny was in intensive care for three weeks, and in a coma for most of it. During this period the rest of our family had time to accept Charlotte's death. We also experienced the healing that came from the love and support of our relatives, friends, and community. Mother commented during this time that it would be much harder for Kenny to accept what had happened since he had not been able to experience it directly as we had. We discussed the fact that when he seemed ready, it would be very important for us to share with him what had happened and how much love and support there had been for him and for our family.

About three weeks after the accident, Kenny began to ask about Charlotte. We shared with him everything that had happened, but our sharing did not seem to accomplish the emotional healing that I had hoped. Perhaps the power of these events was lost in their retelling, or perhaps we discouraged Kenny from grieving over Charlotte's death because we thought it would hurt his recovery. Whatever the reason, Kenny didn't experience the same resolve about Charlotte's death that I did. For years a sense of loss seemed to follow him.

Kenny was in the hospital for three full months undergoing different surgeries—jaw, wrist, femur, and shoulder, but he survived. After a while we became fairly confident that he was going to regain his good health. During that time, I drove back from college frequently to be with him in the hospital, but otherwise I devoted myself completely to my studies.

Seize the Day

I knew after all this that I wanted to go into medicine. As a result, I found it very easy to apply myself so that I could do my best to get the grades required for medical school. Beyond having gained a sense of direction in my schooling, I had also learned a very important lesson. According to medical science and the law of averages, I was supposed to have a short difficult life as a diabetic. Charlotte was supposed to have had a long healthy life.

Charlotte's death illustrated for me in a dramatic way that medical science does not determine how any one life will be. As individuals, our lives do not comply with statistical averages. No one has any guarantee that his or her life or health will last.

I made the decision after Charlotte's death that I was going to live my life more in the present. I decided to make sure that my life, however long or short it might be, was filled with joy and with singing, dancing, and playing, and not so much with building for a distant future.

The Miracle of Healing

Looking back, I realize that I also learned a great deal from Charlotte's death about the healing power of love. When Charlotte died, I was initially overwhelmed with sadness. When I had that feeling, I didn't feel any sense of purpose or joy in living. After initially being overwhelmed by the realization of how much I had lost, I became open to the new recognition that her life still held meaning and joy for me. When friends and family related to me how much they loved Charlotte, I thought of how much I loved her. When I was full of love for Charlotte, my pain over losing her began to diminish. Through my love for her, I began to feel acceptance and meaning in a life without her.

When I think of Charlotte now, I feel great joy and deep appreciation that I was able to be a brother to such a wonderful person. I accept the miracle of having had her in my life.

I recognize now that my love for Kenny and my determination to help him heal also played an important part in helping me heal from losing Charlotte. In order to give Kenny my love and determination for him to live, I had to feel that love and that determination to live inside myself. To keep those feelings strong inside me, I had to give up my despair over Charlotte's death. I couldn't successfully sustain both feelings at a deep level. When I gave my love to Kenny who was comatose and unaware, I was healing myself.

I had heard the saying, "The gift is in the giving," and had not really understood its significance. Now it meant something to me. When I was supportive of those who were having trouble accepting Charlotte's death, I began to feel strong, emotionally mature, and whole. Realizing that I had something to give instilled in me a sense of worth. Giving love and support also made me more attuned to the love and support that was there for me if I needed it.

I believe that in order for any of us to heal ourselves from such losses, we must find in others or within ourselves the love that will sustain us. If we have a reserve of self-love built up within us, then in times of loss we can look within to find healing. If we do not have a very strong sense of self-love, then we need to look to whatever will make us feel the greatest sense of love and use that loving to revive and nurture our own love for ourselves. There are many things that we can use to avoid or distract ourselves from the pain of loss, but I believe that love is the greatest and only true healer.

3

From Edinburgh to Boston

> *Youth is the time to go flashing from one end of the world to the other both in mind and body; to try the manners of different nations; to hear the chimes at midnight; to see sunrise in town and country; to be converted at a revival; to circumnavigate the metaphysics, write halting verses, run a mile to see a fire, and wait all day long in the theatre to applaud "Hernani."*
> — Robert Louis Stevenson, "Crabbed Age and Youth"

After the accident that killed Charlotte and injured Kenny, I knew that I wanted to become a doctor. I wanted never again to feel as helpless as I had felt listening to Kenny scream in Rockford Memorial Hospital's emergency room. Suffering always seemed to touch off a kind of pain inside of me, and I wanted the power to heal suffering. I had always liked our family doctor and felt confidence in his kindly care. The idea of being a family doctor appealed to me.

At the University of Wisconsin, I declared pre-med studies as my major and busied myself by taking required courses. By the end of my sophomore year, I found that I had completed most of my requirements. This meant I could take all elective courses for a year and still graduate on time.

I began to think about studying abroad. The idea of broadening my cultural experience was appealing. Living in a foreign country would give me a feeling of independence and adventure I had not known before. I would be living in a strange environment where the foods, customs, and medical care were all unknowns. This would be an opportunity to further test my limits as a young man living and thriving with diabetes. The challenge and the elements of risk appealed to me. After some research, I finally settled on a program in Edinburgh, Scotland.

The Candy Bar Heresy

Scotland was a land of surprises. When I arrived in Scotland, I had not seen a doctor about my diabetes in several years. Since my student health plan at the University of Wisconsin only provided for illness and injury, I had been in the habit of seeing a doctor only when I was sick.

At my student orientation in Edinburgh, I learned that I, like other diabetics, was expected to visit the local clinic on a regular basis. Because Great Britain had a system of socialized medicine, and I was considered a guest of the country, these visits would be free. Otherwise, I could never have afforded them.

Front flap of my Edinburgh University student ID pass

My first visit to this clinic lasted several hours. During this time, I was given blood and urine tests, I talked with a dietician and nurse, and finally, I discussed the results of the tests and the diet plan with a doctor. With this team treatment, which took place every three or four months, I came to have a much better sense than I'd ever had before of how I was taking care of my diabetes.

Collegiate running was also very different in Scotland than in the States. At the University of Wisconsin, I had not been running competitively because I was not fast enough to make UW's traveling cross-country team. I had just trained by myself and run intramurals. At the University of Edinburgh, running was a club activity, and the focus was more on camaraderie and enjoyment of the sport than on winning. Looking for friendship and fun, I joined the University running club, the Edinburgh "Hare and Hounds."

I was surprised to find that although there was not much competitive pressure, the workouts were much more rigorous than anything I'd been doing. Every day, we ran five or six miles in the physically demanding hill country south of Edinburgh. On weekends, we would often travel to a rustic retreat on the shore of Loch Tay and spend two or three days training. On each of these training days, we would get up and run five or six miles before breakfast. Then we would relax and kayak or play pool until early afternoon when we went through a more extended running workout. After supper, we would run once again.

One of the first things I noticed about these workouts was that my blood sugar regularly dropped to the point where I was hypoglycemic. On one run, I knocked on a farmhouse door and asked for food because I was afraid my blood sugar was so low that I might go into insulin shock. My practice of eating a sandwich and an apple prior to my runs just wasn't giving me the reserves I needed. So the next time I went to the diabetic clinic on one of my regular visits, I asked the doctor for his advice.

"Why don't you just eat a candy bar before you run to raise your sugar," he suggested.

I couldn't believe what I was hearing. Ever since I first learned of my diabetes, I had been operating on the belief that I could never eat a candy bar. I'd been told my body couldn't handle concentrated sweets. Now a Scottish doctor was telling me to eat candy bars!

A candy bar, he said, was a more concentrated sugar source than the sandwiches and apples I had been relying on. With the help of this "sugar-loading" I could keep my sugar level up during a whole five- or six-mile run. It would not be dangerous because I would burn it off running. Although I was uneasy letting go of a belief that I had held for so long, I felt a sense of pleasure and expansion as I broke out of my old mindset and saw that my old rule was not, in fact, an absolute.

By eating a candy bar before running, I found that I was able to keep my blood sugar level up during workouts much more easily than before. I also enjoyed running more without a stomach full of sandwiches.

Our races usually took place on Saturdays. On those mornings, a group of anywhere from seven to fifteen runners would get up at 5:00 a.m. or 6:00 a.m. and catch an early train out of Edinburgh. We would travel an hour or two to Glasgow or Dundee or one of the other towns where we competed. Our running contests would usually take place near a playing field where there were dressing rooms and cold-water showers.

The race itself would cover a distance of about five miles, usually across plowed fields, under barbed wire fences and through streams. We would come back totally covered with mud and exhausted. It was a much more rough-and-tumble kind of running than cross-country running in the U.S., where races were often held on golf courses. After the race we would take a cold shower to get the mud off and then go with the host club to have hot tea and biscuits or soup. Often, we'd also go to a bar for pints of ale, and finally, after a very full day, catch a late train home.

My family doctor at home had always emphasized that anyone with type 1 diabetes should not drink any alcohol. And I had not been drinking any alcohol to speak of prior to my travel to Scotland, but my Scottish doctor at the Edinburgh University diabetes clinic told me that an occasional beer or two would not be any problem as far as my diabetes was concerned. (First the candy bars, and now beer drinking—clearly higher education was good for me!) So, when the team went to the pub for ale, I joined right in.

I drank moderately because I knew beer was high in calories, and because I never wanted to have so much alcohol that I wasn't paying attention to my blood sugar. I was young and healthy and did not, at this point, feel any negative side effects from drinking. Years later, however, I began to notice a feeling of mental and physical sluggishness when I drank, and I eventually gave it up altogether.

I was the 10th or 11th fastest runner in the Edinburgh club. Only the top five runners counted for purposes of competition, but we felt our successes were very much a team effort. We didn't even have a coach. Our coaching consisted of talking among ourselves about what worked well and what didn't. Club sports seemed like a polar opposite of scholastic sports in the U.S., where college athletes often had trainers, coaches, and doctors, along with all of the pressures of a professional athlete. When I think of running purely for the joy of it, I think of Edinburgh.

Making it through the physically demanding weekend workouts at Loch Tay gave me confidence that I could probably do other things that I had felt unsure about, like traveling. During school vacations I began to do quite a bit of hitchhiking, eventually making my way all over northern Europe. I took my insulin with me and kept in good diabetic control as I traveled. I also carried bread and cheese with me at all times so that I never had to worry about low blood sugar. I was delighted to find that I could travel as far and as cheaply as any of my school friends.

The sense of freedom and discovery I felt as I traveled really strengthened my belief that I could do whatever I really wanted to do, regardless of my diabetes. I saw that some of the rules I had been given as a patient with diabetes were unnecessarily limiting. I was beginning to see rules differently than before and feeling much less inclined to follow them blindly. If I understood the purpose for any given rule, I reasoned, I could determine whether it was right for me and whether there might be better ways to achieve the underlying objective.

Squeeze Bottles

When I returned to Wisconsin for my senior year of college, 1971–1972, I was in such good condition from my "Hare and Hounds" training that I decided to try out for the University cross-country team as a "walk-on," meaning that I was not a known or recruited athlete, and I would have to prove my skills. In the team time trials I was the eighth or ninth fastest runner, which meant that although I would not be on the traveling team, I would be able to compete in all of the home meets.

The coach was very supportive of me as a runner and even volunteered to carry the honey that I took to "sugar-load" before meets. After a few episodes where my honey leaked all over his gear, he gave me the honey back and let me know he wouldn't be carrying it anymore. Initially, I interpreted this to mean that I wasn't important to him. But after a bit more thought I realized that my coach's willingness to put up with honey all over his gear was not a reliable measure of my importance to the team.

During my senior year at college, I decided to try running in the next Boston Marathon, to be held on Monday, April 17, 1973. This race is the world's oldest annual marathon and ranks as one of the major marathons in the country. It was also farther than I'd ever run before by ten or fifteen miles. It seemed like a good next step in testing my limits.

As a happy hippie, circa 1973

As I began to train for the marathon, I realized that eating a candy bar prior to the race would not give me enough sugar to run more than twenty-six miles. I would need to have something during the race itself. I tried carrying candy bars with me on the run but found them less than ideal. Not only did they melt into a mess, but I found it very difficult to swallow these gooey globs while running.

Looking for another energy source, I began to experiment with drinking a sugar water solution as I ran. I would carry a small plastic squeeze bottle, filled with eight ounces of water, about ten teaspoons of sugar, a little lemon or lime juice for taste, and a pinch of salt, and drink from it whenever I felt the need for more sugar. I did this totally by feel since the glucose monitor, a device for measuring blood sugar, had not yet been developed. Since I was running forty to seventy miles a week for training, I had plenty of opportunities to test my concoction. I found that one bottle would last about five miles.

Although Gatorade® had been developed in 1965 for athletes, I was experimenting with a formula to specifically help me with blood sugar control. Gatorade® simply didn't have enough sugar in it for my purpose.

I also experimented with reducing the amount of insulin I was giving myself before a run to compensate for the amount of exercise. The combination of sipping sugar water and reducing my insulin seemed to give me a consistent physical boost for workouts. I was excited at the success of these running experiments and at the sense of personal discovery. I was learning that much more was possible for me than I'd ever imagined.

"Go, Farnland!"

Since I figured I would need about forty ounces of sugar water, or five bottles, to complete the marathon, I planned out a system where I could trade off for a new water bottle every five miles along the marathon course. My brother Kenny

Kenny wearing a Farnland T-shirt at Weeona Lake

offered to drive to each of the five-mile checkpoints and hand me a new sugar water bottle as I came through.

After Kenny had fully recovered from his injuries from the car accident and graduated from high school, he went off to college at the University of Minnesota in Minneapolis. I was about a four-hour drive away in Madison, Wisconsin, but we stayed in close touch and saw each other regularly at family gatherings at the lake cabin. He was eager to support me in my first marathon. My brother Stephen and I also remained close, but he was too busy to be my water boy.

Stephen at Weeona Lake in Central Wisconsin

In 1961, my parents joined forces with two of Dad's cousins and one of those cousin's parents to buy a 160-acre forested track of land that surrounded a 12-acre lake. The four families got together and agreed on the name Weeona Lake, since we laughed every time we talked about it: "We own a lake!" After some years of tent camping, we built a cabin on the lake, and of course, named it Weeona Cabin. There was only one road leading into the lake across our property, so it was truly a private piece of paradise. Our community of family and friends made up the name "Farnland" to call this special out-of-the-way part of the world.

We also created our own language, our own national flag, and even fun summer clothes to wear at the lake, like the pastel shorts in the Farnland colors, half pink and half baby blue. We created a different T-shirt every year, and for at least ten years we gave an award every Fourth of July weekend to the person who did the most to promote Farnland.

I decided to promote our community by wearing my pink and baby blue Farnland shorts and matching shirt for the Boston Marathon, a popular and well-publicized race.

When the day of the marathon arrived, I was in good shape and well prepared. I had the sense that everything would go smoothly. One of the real pleasures of that marathon was running through Wellesley College, an all-girls private college, which was the halfway point. The girls came out en masse to cheer the runners, crowding in on both sides of the raceway and forming a narrow chute of one or two yards. They used whatever was written on a runner's T-shirt as their cheering cue. In my case it was "Go, Farnland!"

As I came into this cheering human chute, I felt tremendous exhilaration from their support and found myself sprinting for 200 yards all the way down the chute. After 200 yards the people began to thin out again, and I realized I still had thirteen miles to go. The Wellesleyans had given me, nonetheless, a boost that stayed with me for the rest of the run.

At the finish line, the reception was even greater. The crowd literally roared as I came in. My time of three hours and twenty-seven minutes, about eight minutes per mile, was not exceptional, but the tremendous feeling of approval and appreciation I got from the cheering crowd made me feel like a homecoming hero. This wonderful reception was given to every runner.

After the race, we went to the Prudential Center to recover. It looked like a war zone. There were bodies everywhere—people lying on cots getting fluids replaced and runners coming in for hours and hours after the race. There was a beef stew being served, which seemed totally unappealing to me.

There was also a tremendous feeling of accomplishment and sense of belonging.

Buoyed by this tremendous experience, I decided to run the Boston Marathon every year. I wanted to feel the things I'd felt at the event on a regular basis—the sense of my own physical ability in completing one of the most grueling races in the country, the sense of camaraderie I felt as one of this healthy, upbeat, group of marathoners, and the sense of approval that I felt from within and without.

A New Tradition

Competing in the annual Boston Marathon became a tradition for me, and I ran it for nine years consecutively, from 1973–1981.

One particularly hot year, I found myself getting so tired and dehydrated and achy early in the race that I could hardly keep running. Recognizing that my body was sending me a message, I dropped out of the race at the eleven-mile marker.

I immediately tested my sugar level on a urine strip I had in my car. My sugar level was very, very high. I had misjudged the sugar-to-water ratio of my solution given the extreme heat. I was getting too little water and too much sugar. The more I

My fastest run of the Boston Marathon April 16, 1979

tried to rehydrate myself with the water in the sugar solution, the higher my blood sugar went also.

This kind of imbalance problem with my diabetes was rare, however. Of the thirty marathons I ran in the decade after my senior year of college, there were only two that I did not finish.

My times in the Boston Marathon continued to improve dramatically. By 1979 I knew the Boston racecourse quite well, and I was in my best running condition ever. During the nervous pre-race warmup of that race, I sensed that I would do quite well. I ran my first mile in five minutes and forty seconds, which was much faster than my first mile in any previous marathon. At each mile marker, I calculated my average time per mile and was delighted to find that I was running consistently under six minutes per mile. I knew well before the halfway point that I was having a great race.

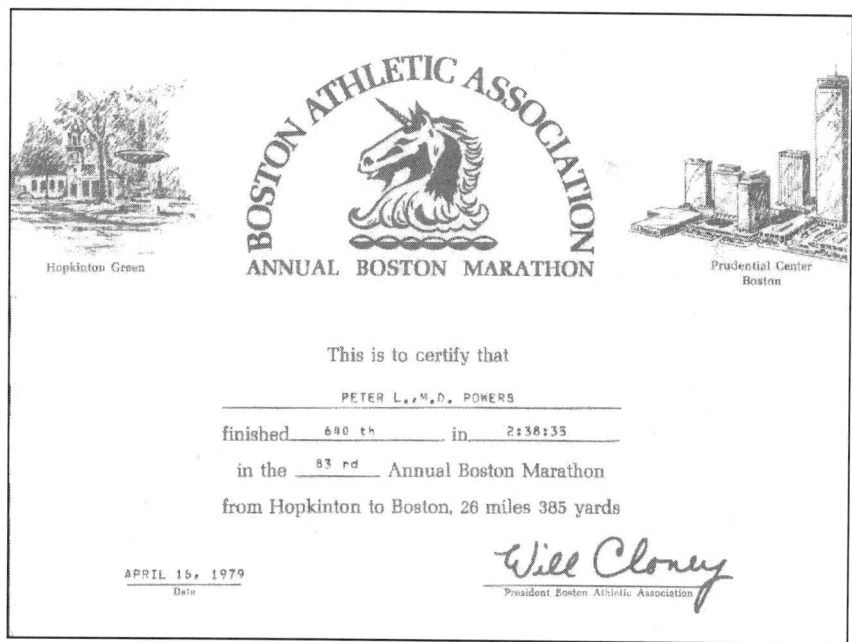

My time of 2:38:35 for this race distance was an average of 6 minutes and 3 seconds per mile.

By the time I reached the Newton Hills, and the famous "Heartbreak Hill," I was so excited about my speed that I felt none of the mental resistance that can overcome a runner in these hills. Coming out of the hills after the twenty-mile marker, I accelerated into my last six miles. I finished in two hours and thirty-eight minutes, having run an average of six minutes and three seconds per mile, shaving almost a full hour off my first Boston Marathon time.

The finish of this race is still one of the most vivid memories of my life. I can still see the faces in the crowd, hear their cheers, taste the warm sweat trickling down my face, and feel the excitement of having run the best race of my life. I was the 640th finisher of 7000 runners in one of the toughest races in the country. As I slowed down to a walk, I basked in a wonderful feeling of pride, success, and appreciation that came both from within myself and from those around me.

After the marathon, I met Dr. George Sheehan, a cardiologist and noted running expert, and he took great interest in the fact that I was diabetic. He pointed out that my times were exceptional. By his unofficial tally, I was the fastest marathoner with diabetes in the U.S. At that time, I imagine there were very few marathoners in the U.S. with diabetes. Although I had been aware that I was exploring new territory in terms of my own capabilities, I had not previously thought in terms of my running being of interest to anyone else. Dr. Sheehan pointed out that I could do a lot to change the belief that exercise is harmful for people with diabetes.

Dr. Sheehan and I corresponded for several years after our meeting, and he would refer questions to me he received about running with diabetes. I wrote a lot of letters to aspiring diabetic marathoners. Eventually, I began writing magazine articles for publications for runners and for people with diabetes.

I enjoyed contradicting the common notion that people with diabetes can't enjoy robust health, vigorous exercise, and involvement in athletic sports. In giving running advice, I would stress not only the importance of keeping one's blood sugar levels balanced *during* a race but in keeping good diabetic control during the training period when one is actually building and storing the fuel *for* the race. Extending this idea, I suggested that regular good attention to one's own needs and health was a good framework for lifelong health and happiness.

Pushing the "Envelope"

After having run some two dozen marathons, including multiple Boston Marathons, I began to think about stretching myself further. I had heard of a new running event, the ultramarathon, a race of fifty miles, about which I felt both excited and incredulous.

The marathon, a 26.2-mile race, had always been considered the ultimate long-distance event. Now people were running twice that distance. I knew when I first heard about it that I wanted to run it. I would be doing something that most people would never dream of doing. Not only would I be proving to myself that I wasn't limited by my diabetes, but I would be doing something that most people couldn't do. I wouldn't just be keeping up; I would be stepping ahead.

The ultramarathon I chose was an annual British race from London to Brighton, a small town on the English coast. The race I ran was held in the fall of 1979. As part of my training, I did a bicycle tour of Scotland and England with my girlfriend at the time, Hetty. We cycled about forty to sixty miles a day, and I would also go out on training runs each day. We stayed at bed and breakfast lodgings along the way so that we were well rested. I felt very healthy.

My relationship with Hetty eventually ended although at the time I felt like I was in love and would be with her indefinitely. I know now, but didn't know then, that I shied away from commitment because I was afraid of making a mistake. When things got too close in a relationship, it tended to end. My relationship with Hetty was one of many that similarly and eventually fell apart after six to eighteen months.

The bicycle trip with Hetty affirmed again that I could do whatever I set my mind to in spite of my diabetes. I could bicycle for three weeks through a foreign country, eat properly, take my insulin properly, keep my blood sugar levels well regulated, and be really healthy. On top of that I could even train for an athletic event.

Hetty was my support team for the race. Here, my special sugar drinks were not an oddity. Most ultramarathoners were using such drinks to help them go long distances. I just drank a lot more than the others. Where most people had two or three special drink bottles spread out along the course, I had nine or ten. During the race Hetty rode in the bus with the other support people and made sure that my bottles were where I needed them.

The race was scheduled to begin at 7:00 a.m. at the Tower of Big Ben in the center of London. The race started on the first stroke of the hour bell, and I felt ecstatic. I had a hard time believing I was actually going to run fifty miles, and it felt exhilarating to be making the attempt.

The racecourse was very hilly, and it wound down through the countryside to Brighton. This race did not have hundreds

I kept pace with Leslie Watson for much of the race in the 1979 50-mile ultramarathon from London to Brighton.

of thousands of spectators like the Boston Marathon. Along much of the course there were no spectators at all, and the runners were so spread out that I went for miles at a time without seeing or hearing another person. The rewards in this race were mostly internal—knowing you were doing something amazing and being proud of yourself for doing it.

There were a lot of European runners in the race and six or eight American runners. Much of the race I ran with Leslie Watson who was, at the time, the world record holder for women in the fifty-mile run.

After I had run about twenty-six miles, I began to notice that I wasn't "hitting the wall." This is a running term that refers to an almost insurmountable fatigue and muscle soreness that a runner feels after a certain distance. I never hit the wall. I kept thinking, "How can this be? I'm running twice the distance of a marathon, and I don't feel any different than when I run a marathon." I later learned that after twenty-six miles, a runner's additional fatigue is usually so gradual that it is barely perceptible. A runner will feel the same at thirty miles or forty miles or fifty miles as at twenty-six miles.

As I neared the town of Brighton, I began to feel the same exhilaration I had experienced when the race began. I finished 42nd in a field of 141 runners, with a time of six hours fifty-three minutes—an average pace of seven minutes and thirty-five seconds per mile. I had accomplished a physical feat that was amazing, not just for a diabetic but for any athlete. I felt incredible! There was an awards ceremony after the race where the Lord Provost of Brighton handed out medals and awards. By this time, I was feeling little short of invincible.

As soon as the ultramarathon was over, Hetty and I talked about her desire to go home early. We had planned another week in England to travel together but she was missing her two young boys so much that she wanted to go home. I realized that if we went back to the U.S. a week early, I could make it to my sister Ellen's wedding in Aspen, Colorado, so we hopped on a plane.

I think of this ultramarathon when I want to remember what it feels like to feel really successful. I use this memory as a tool when I need an extra push to do something that is really important to me. I go back in my mind to Brighton and feel that excitement, that feeling of power, and I realize that I can feel that again. This gives me confidence and makes me more effective.

Another personal success that meant a lot to me was being voted as the most outstanding student in a vote among all the teachers at my high school. I was not the valedictorian, and I wasn't the school's greatest athlete, but I really appreciated being recognized by the teachers and staff.

Building on memories of a success in this way can be a useful tool for anyone. Even if a person feels a lack of accomplishment, he or she can start by using the memory of small successes to build confidence.

Success tends to build upon success. Successes help us to feel good about ourselves, and they help us learn to value activities that give us happiness over ones that give us approval.

4

Gross Anatomy

> "And hast thou slain the Jabberwock? Come to my arms, my beamish boy! O frabjous day! Callooh! Callay!" He chortled in his joy.
> —Lewis Carroll, "Jabberwocky" in *Through the Looking Glass*

Getting into medical school was, and still is, a very competitive process. I knew that it would not be easy. But I saw medicine as my life's calling, and I dismissed the possibility that something might keep me from that mission. I held to the belief that getting accepted to medical school was just a question of where and when. I felt I had a good chance of being admitted to the University of Wisconsin medical school. It had a good reputation, but it was not one of the most competitive schools. My grades and my Medical College Admission Test scores were adequate but not high enough to be assured of being admitted.

At that time the medical school at the University of Wisconsin did not require a personal interview. But I wanted an interview. I was looking for something to tip the balance. I thought of myself as likeable, and I felt that an interview would increase my chances of being admitted. I requested an interview and got it.

I met with the dean of admissions, a doctor, who knew from my application that I had diabetes. He had already determined before our interview that I would not be admitted because of my diabetes, and he was very straightforward in telling me this. He didn't see anything questionable about his determination. In fact, he felt his decision was dictated by sound public policy.

There were two stacks of applications on the dean's desk, and my application had been placed in the reject pile. The lack of consideration for my healthy lifestyle and athleticism was obviously unfair and prejudiced. But I kept calm in the face of this rejection and felt grateful I had followed my instincts to ask for an interview. This at least gave me the chance to argue for a different outcome.

"As a diabetic you have a much shorter life expectancy than the average person," the dean told me. "It doesn't make sense for the state to train you if you are only going to practice medicine for fifteen or twenty years when we can train someone else who is likely to practice for forty or fifty years."

At the time there were no federal or state laws prohibiting this type of discrimination on the basis of personal disability. This was 1972, and the American Disabilities Act wasn't passed until 1990. I had only logic and the force of my convictions to rely upon.

I told him that his reasoning didn't make sense. No medical student signs an agreement to stay in practice for a given length of time. No medical student signs an agreement to live a healthy safe life. If statistical probabilities were really at issue, then medical school admittees would be signing agreements to remain in the profession and abstain from smoking, high cholesterol diets, skydiving, and similar dangerous pursuits.

I said that if anyone deserved a chance to practice medicine based on his commitment to maintaining good health, it was me. I told the dean in detail about my history of good health, good diabetic control, and marathon running. I also told him about my very strong intention to go to medical school and practice medicine. I told him how much I had admired the doctor who had treated our family when I was growing up. I talked about how much I felt this doctor had affected my life by advising me that I didn't need to be limited by my diabetes, contrary to the prevailing medical belief at the time. I said I wanted to do for others what my doctor had done for me and my family. I wanted very much to be a family doctor.

I'm not sure that the dean ever changed his mind about the policy considerations he had discussed with me, but he did change his mind about me. I was admitted to medical school at the University of Wisconsin!

Give and Take

I believe that I was accepted into medical school because I was willing to stand up for myself and make a good case for my admission. I didn't get angry or attack the dean personally for his beliefs. I just wasn't willing to take "no" for an answer. This was a great lesson for me. It taught me not to be discouraged by opposing viewpoints or to accept an authoritative decision as final.

This doesn't take away from the importance of listening to others and to be open to their points of view. For example, the dean of admissions knew a lot more about medical school than I did, and there may have been very valid reasons why medical school would not have been right for me. But the dean didn't know as much about diabetes as I did or why I would have made an excellent doctor in spite of—or even because of—my condition.

If I had automatically assumed that the dean's opinion was more valid than my own, I would have lost a tremendous opportunity. And society and the medical profession would have lost all that I had to offer as a physician during the years I practiced medicine. It is easy to fall into a pattern where we either believe that other people are always right, or we refuse to listen to others at all. I think the key is in being truly open to all points of view, including one's own.

Running the Gauntlet

Medical school was more than just a rigorous and challenging training period. In some respects, it could also be thought of as a grueling hazing for those entering the profession. During our first two years, we took classes continuously from 7:45 a.m. to 5:00 p.m. with an hour off for lunch. That was the equivalent of a full-time job. But class time was only an opener. For each hour of class, we were also expected to do two hours of reading outside of class. That didn't leave time in the day for anything else, not even sleep.

The reading assignments were overwhelming. They covered the entire scope of modern medicine:

Biochemistry • Cardiology • Dermatology •
Endocrinology • Gastroenterology •
Genito-urinary systems • Gynecology •
Gross anatomy • Hematology • Immunology •
Medical statistics • Microbiology •
Musculo-skeletal systems • Nephrology •
Neuro-anatomy • Neurology • Obstetrics • Oncology •
Ophthalmology • Orthopedics • Otolaryngology •
Pediatrics • Pharmacology • Physiology •
Pulmonary systems • Radiology

Most students studied five or six hours a night. This meant that they were trying to concentrate very intensely for about fourteen hours a day.

I knew this amount of concentration wasn't possible. At least it was not possible to do it in a sustained healthy way. Early on I decided to do two things to keep myself together under this pressure. First, I decided to keep running. I figured I would actually be further ahead by taking the time to run since running would refresh me emotionally and mentally. Every day at noon I would run five miles. Then I would eat my lunch during the first afternoon lecture. Often I would be so tense following the afternoon lectures that I would run again before dinner.

Even though running refreshed and invigorated me, I still knew I couldn't absorb everything that was being presented. So I decided that rather than wearing myself out by endless studying, I would limit the amount of time I spent studying and try to be more effective in the time allotted. The decision to limit my study time was a hard one for me. I was a very competitive person. I knew that limiting my study time meant that I would not graduate at or near the top of the class.

The top graduates were the ones who would be accepted for the best residency programs at the top university hospitals. The most competitive of these were the ones who would become teachers and researchers at the more prestigious medical institutions. I knew that what I really wanted to do was work with people, to be a family doctor.

Graduating at the top of my class or teaching at Harvard or Johns Hopkins University would not necessarily increase my opportunities to work with families. And it was clear that the time I would have to invest to be truly competitive would mean that I wouldn't be able to enjoy many of the other things in life that I really valued. Graduating at the top of the class would have been a nice achievement, but the price I would have had to pay was too high.

I decided to accept the fact that I would be in the middle of the class ranking and not at the top. I knew I was intelligent and capable, and I decided not to make my grades a measure of my ability or worth. It wasn't always easy to hold back from trying to prove myself to my classmates and professors. Sometimes it was also difficult to refrain from judging myself. But I determined to do my best to set my own standards for achievement and be happy with them.

I committed myself to two hours of high-quality study time every day. If I got distracted or took time out to talk or go for coffee, that time didn't count. To help motivate myself, I played a little game.

Before studying I would shower and dress up as if I were going out on a date. On my way to study I would walk down State Street in Madison where lots of people would be out window shopping, going to coffee houses, and listening to music. There was a lot of high-spiritedness and good energy on State Street, and as I walked, I felt a part of it. This reinforced the feeling that I was doing something fun.

I didn't study in the medical school library because the atmosphere there was too tense. Instead, I went to the student union or the undergraduate library or one of the chapels where it was comfortable and quiet. After studying for two hours, I still usually had a little time to hang out at the student union and have a snack before going home.

Through this approach I was actually able to create the upbeat feeling that I was "going out" instead of being burdened by the feeling that I was "going to study." It made me feel I was having a full life instead of enduring drudgery for some future reward. This made studying itself a lot more enjoyable and productive.

Trade-offs

Comparing my experience with that of some of my classmates, I found that my approach worked relatively well. Many of the students who graduated at the top of the class did not seem very happy. Even though they had done very well, they worried that they had not done better. For them, more competition and stress loomed ahead—residency placements, faculty and research appointments, and career success.

A good friend of mine dropped out of school in our third year. He believed that he wasn't smart enough or compassionate enough or good enough to be a doctor. Although his grades were quite adequate, he had overwhelmed himself by thinking that he had to be at the top of the class.

When I think of this friend, I am reminded of a joke that went around during school: Question: "What do you call the medical student who graduates at the bottom of the class?" Answer: "Doctor."

The point is that it is the basic competence to practice medicine that counts in the professional world, not relative performance in medical school. My friend's grades were average, but he would have made an excellent doctor. Even if he had graduated at the bottom of the class, he would still have been a capable doctor. But he told himself that being average was not good enough.

Obviously, there is only one place at the top of the class. If being number one in the class is the only achievement that is good enough, then medical schools should admit only one person per class. Of course that would be absurd. Unfortunately, many of us impose expectations upon ourselves that are equally illogical.

I remember very vividly the experience of another student in our class who made a choice similar to mine. She was a woman approaching the end of her childbearing years. She wanted to be in medical school, and yet she also wanted to have a child. She conceived and had her baby at the same time she went to medical school. She brought the child to class and nursed it during lectures.

When I watched her cradle her infant with one arm and take notes with the other, I had tremendous respect and great admiration for the priorities she had established. Graduating at the top of the class and getting a prestigious residency were clearly not the most critical things in her life. Despite pressure from her classmates and professors, she had decided not to make medical school her first priority.

I was profoundly affected by her example. It reinforced my own resolve to honor the choice I had made to stay healthy and happy during my training.

I realize now that there are always choices in what we do. If I had a tendency to feel overwhelmed by the curriculum in medical school, that was a choice I had made. If I felt that my life was out of balance and that I didn't have time to relax and enjoy myself, that was also a choice.

On Call

The third and fourth years of medical school are spent doing clinical rotations or clerkships. This consists of following a doctor around a hospital or clinic and learning how to do what doctors do.

During my clerkship, I was on duty for about ten hours a day and was on call every third night. If someone came into the hospital needing treatment while I was on call, I didn't get to sleep. The University of Wisconsin medical school, like most university hospitals, was understaffed. The hospital administration seemed to rely on the long hours required of the medical students as a way to make both ends of the budget meet.

My rotations were at first both exciting and intimidating. On one occasion I removed the dressing from the wound of a patient who had been treated by our supervising surgeon. I thought this would be the best way to inspect for infection. When the surgeon found out, he chewed me out in front of the other students like a military drill sergeant.

"Don't you ever touch a dressing I have made," he scolded. "You have wasted my time. If anything like this ever happens again, you will no longer be at this hospital!"

At the time I felt ashamed and upset even though what I had done was not careless or dangerous. In fact, it was a perfectly appropriate procedure. But after I was reprimanded, I felt that somehow I should have known beforehand not to do what I had done.

Now I realize that this surgeon was probably using me to unload whatever frustrations he had been carrying around at the time. I had made a reasonable decision, and there was no cause for me to have taken the incident personally.

I also had my successes. On one of the wards where I worked there was a wealthy, eccentric, and difficult patient. He needed regular shots to thin a dangerous blood clot in his leg, but he was deathly afraid of needles. He had become so abusive with the nurses that I was finally sent to deal with him.

I sensed immediately that I could help this man because I remembered my own initial fear of shots. I introduced myself and told him that I had diabetes. I told him that I had given myself at least two shots a day for the last ten years and that he was unlikely to ever meet anyone who knew as much about giving shots as I did. I told him that I was so skilled at giving shots that I could give him a shot that he would not even feel. This man was taken in enough to let me try, and he was amazed at the result. After that he refused to let anyone but me give him his shots.

There had been one prior situation where my familiarity with needles was an advantage. The very first time as medical students we were told we had to practice drawing blood from each other for lab work, a number of my friends only wanted me to do the honors for them. We were all intimidated by the idea of a total novice sticking a big needle into our arms, so my experience stuck me with more than my fair share of practice needlesticks.

Although it disrupted the hospital routine when I had to be called away from other duties to tend to this eccentric shot-fearing patient, it did reinforce in me a real sense of accomplishment and importance. Ever since I was a teenager, I had thought of my diabetes as a handicap. This was the first time I had ever experienced diabetes as giving me an advantage.

This was an extraordinary perspective for me. My diabetes had given me a special understanding and skill that many people did not have. This enabled me to help some patients in ways that other doctors could not.

After I began practicing medicine, I understood how my diabetes turned out to be a very real blessing. As a physician I was called upon to be a healer. Since I had experienced illness, pain, and physical limitations, I could better understand my patients' responses to illness, pain, and loss. I was more understanding, more insightful, and more compassionate in dealing with patients than if I'd never had diabetes.

Eventually I learned that in almost every disappointment or hurt there is also an opportunity. I experienced this with my diabetes, but this principle can be applied to most physical disabilities.

For example, men in their forties or fifties who have experienced a heart attack often view this setback as a great tragedy. In order to restore their health, they generally have to make very basic changes in their lives. They give up smoking; they start to exercise; they diet to lose weight, and then start making healthier food choices. They reduce their workload or change jobs to do something that is less stressful or more personally meaningful, and they decide to spend more time with family and loved ones. Almost invariably these men find their new lives to be much richer and more satisfying than the lives they were living before their heart conditions forced them to make changes.

The Miracle of Life

As a medical student I began to experience many aspects of life that had, until then, been closed to my view. The first time I helped deliver a baby, I was extremely nervous and tense. I felt that what I was doing was so important that I didn't want to make any mistakes. I had a compulsion to keep asking the supervising doctor if I was doing everything right. I really had to bite my tongue because I knew such questions would probably upset the expectant mother. When we were done, I again had to bite my tongue because the new parents were so grateful and thanked me so profusely, and I felt that I had really just been learning at their expense.

Since then, I've delivered over 300 babies, and every single birth was like experiencing a miracle. When the baby was finally born, I would feel this tremendous release of anxiety and anticipation. I also felt overwhelming joy when I placed the infant on the mother's breast to nurse. At those times I felt so close and bonded to the parents and the little person that had come into the world that I would often have the same tears of joy that the parents did.

Delivering a baby made me realize how interconnected all people are in a deeply spiritual way. Those were the moments when I said to myself, "This is why I am a doctor." Those were the times that filled me up and sustained me through other times that were difficult and draining.

Drawing the Line

Medical school was challenging and exciting, but there were costs attached to the way I was being trained. Being on call made it difficult for me to keep my blood sugar properly regulated. I had previously been taking a mixture of regular insulin and a slower-acting insulin. The regular insulin was effective almost immediately, peaked about three hours after injection, and had a duration of about eight hours. The slower-acting insulin took effect just as rapidly, peaked about eight hours after injection, and could last for up to sixteen hours. By mixing insulins I could obtain the right balance to regulate my blood sugar effectively.

When I was on call, I never knew when I would have time to eat. I had to rely mostly on the fast-acting insulin and take it only when I sat down to eat something. That way I wouldn't have extra insulin lowering my blood sugar when I wasn't able to take the time to eat. But without the intermediate-acting insulin, it was very difficult to keep my blood sugar from taking wide swings.

Like the other medical students, I experienced the fatigue and stress of working long hours on call with little sleep. But when my blood sugar was low, I felt an even greater degree of fatigue, hunger, and irritability. When my blood sugar got too high, I felt flu-like symptoms of aching muscles and exhaustion. My fluctuating blood sugar metabolism also caused me to feel nervous and panicky a lot of the time.

Ultimately, I felt so stressed that I wasn't sure I could make it through the internship. But instead of asking for much needed changes in my schedule, I criticized myself for not keeping better blood sugar control. At some level I still believed that in order to be as good as everyone else, I had to do what they did. I was committed to being a good doctor so I could help others, but I never considered that this meant I had to take care of myself. I never asked myself how ill I was willing to make myself in order to help others. As a result, I pushed myself too far.

Eventually I came to realize that if I didn't take care of myself, I couldn't help others. The obvious reason for this is that if I was ill, I wasn't physically able to assist others. But there is a more fundamental reason. Example is the most powerful teacher. That is true in medicine as it is in other areas of life. I couldn't effectively teach something that I didn't practice. If patients came to me who were making themselves ill with unhealthy stressful lifestyles, I couldn't be very persuasive in advising them to change if I was doing those same things. I had to nurture and take good care of myself if I expected others to learn from me.

Residency

Medical school graduates were required to do a residency, a kind of medical apprenticeship. The first year of this residency was called an internship. After completing the internship, the graduate received a medical license and was free to begin practicing medicine as a general practitioner. The alternative was to complete a three-, four-, or five-year postgraduate residency in a particular specialty.

At the time I completed medical school, about 90 percent of the medical students in the country were doing these three- to five-year residencies. I knew I could go out and practice after my internship, but I wanted the extra training to certify as a family practitioner, which is one of the medical specialties. This would give me more training and make me more qualified than a general practitioner. Looking for a change of scenery after eight years at the University of Wisconsin at Madison, I decided to do my residency at the University of Kentucky in Lexington.

The first year of my residency was one of the worst years of my life. We routinely worked to the point of physical and emotional exhaustion.

First-year residents averaged 110 hours per week working in the hospital. To understand what an exhausting schedule that is, consider that there are only 168 hours total in a week. Every third night I was on call, which meant that I almost always worked through the night with no sleep. Then I would go right on working the next day. With so little sleep it was difficult just to stay awake.

Our internship pay was $9,500 a year. For 110 hours per week, that came out to $1.66 per hour. That was less than half of what teenagers were making at the time working at fast food restaurants.

Like most university hospitals, the hospital at the University of Kentucky didn't hire enough staff to handle its workload. This meant that medical students and residents had to do whatever the hospital staff didn't do. In addition to treating patients, we transported patients, gave x-rays, drew blood, started intravenous lines, administered medication, and performed urinalysis and blood tests. These are all things that nurses, orderlies, lab technicians, and other staff should have been doing.

It wasn't that we were above doing these more routine tasks. The problem was that we were stretched so thin that it was difficult to do all these things and be good doctors, too.

I remember delivering as many as twelve or thirteen babies in one night. Even now I have trouble believing that this would even be possible.

During our surgical rotations we would be in the hospital working for thirty-six hours at a stretch. Then we would have twelve hours off and then come back for another thirty-six-hour stretch.

I remember being so tired that sometimes I would fall asleep while writing on a patient's chart. Several times I was awakened by my pen poking me in the forehead as I nodded off. I found myself nodding off while I was helping with surgery, and I was terrified that I might fall asleep while in the middle of a procedure.

I tried everything I could think of to make myself stay awake. I would walk in place, talk to myself, or try to think of something that would excite or energize me. I would pinch myself on the thigh or cheek so that the pain would keep me more alert. I would even get angry at myself and accuse myself of risking injury to the life and health of my patients. I thought maybe I could threaten myself into staying awake. But that didn't seem to work much better than anything else.

What my body needed was sleep. Sleep was the only thing that would ensure that I could perform my duties in an alert, competent manner. But the medical residency system at that time didn't work that way.

Just as it was during my rotations in medical school, I had to take multiple daily doses of short-acting insulin just before eating instead of following a more regular and effective regimen. This aggravated the exhaustion, anxiousness, and burnout I felt from being so overextended. I believe that my diabetes made this schedule harder for me than for most of the other residents, but I don't think any of them liked it any more than I did.

A month before the end of my first year of residency, I was overwhelmed and near the point of nervous breakdown. I thought that maybe the dean of admissions to the medical school in Wisconsin had been thinking of this grueling schedule when he questioned admitting me to medical school, and maybe he had been right.

One day I was walking home with a fellow resident, and I told him how exhausted and discouraged I was. I said I felt I was failing my patients and that maybe I should drop out of the program.

He told me that I was doing fine and that I always appeared to others as being cheerful and upbeat. I finally broke down sobbing, and he held me quietly until I was done.

This compassion from a fellow resident, who was experiencing the same long hours and sleepless nights as I was, taught me how important the care and understanding of another person can be to someone who is struggling with fear and self-doubt.

Remembering how deeply this experience affected me helped me to return that same level of compassion to my patients. I also learned that the anguish someone may be feeling on the inside doesn't always show up on the outside.

Making Allowances

I made it to the end of my first year of residency, but I was emotionally drained and physically ill. We were only allowed one week off each year, but I knew I couldn't go straight back to this type of a routine. I told the program administrators that I needed a month off. For the first time in my life, I used my diabetes as a justification for special consideration.

I had agonized over that decision. I desperately needed a rest, and I was quite sure that I would not get it without a medical reason. I thought it was very ironic that I was in training to promote good health, and yet my own training program wouldn't give me a month off so that I could stay in good emotional and physical health.

I had never wanted to use my diabetes as an excuse. It was a rule I had made for myself as a teenager. I had never said, "I can't do that because I have diabetes." I didn't want to be making excuses. I just wanted to get better and be healthy again.

As I grew older my refusal to use my diabetes as an excuse was for new reasons. I wanted to prove that I was as good as anyone else. I had to show that I could take anything that anyone else could dish out. I wasn't willing to acknowledge that my diabetes had any effect on my physical ability. I resented having to break the rule to get time off from medical training in my residency, but I didn't see any other way.

My approach to all of this changed over the years to become something quite different. If raising the fact that I had diabetes would get me something that I needed, I had no hesitation in raising it. I came to believe that accepting my physical limitations was an important part of self-acceptance. I learned I could live a full life and still make allowances for who I was.

I was given the month off, but the administrators emphasized that I was allowed this time only because of my diabetes. I went to Aspen, Colorado and spent the time with my sister Ellen. We hiked and camped, and I ran, but I also spent a lot of time just relaxing and resting. This was a wonderful time for me, and during that month I was able to recover a sense of emotional balance and good spirits.

Running in Aspen, Colorado

The second and third years of my residency were still very demanding, but by then we were working about 85 hours a week instead of 110. My schedule was not totally out of control as it had been my first year, and I was able to do a much better job of regulating my blood sugar. During my third year I was chosen to be the chief resident, which meant that I supervised other residents and assisted the faculty in various ways.

I finished my residency in 1979 and received my specialist certification. I was now board certified in family practice. At last, I was what I had wanted to be for so many years, a family doctor.

The Healing Arts

When I look back at my medical training, I think that in some ways I became a good doctor in spite of it and not because of it. There is no question that my training was designed to give me excellent technical skills. But one cannot merely have good technical skills and be a good doctor. Compassion, sensitivity, and the ability to counsel effectively are the hallmarks of effective physicians. I learned these in spite of my training and not because of it. Compassion and sensitivity are extinguished by stress, and the stress of medical training may therefore explain, in part, the inability of many physicians to relate well to patients and co-workers.

This problem is not unique to the medical profession. Many professions and professional training programs do not encourage a balance between acquiring technical skills and sustaining good emotional health. Finding that balance is an important challenge for all of us.

5

The Maroon Bells

May God bless and keep you always
May your wishes all come true
May you always do for others
And let others do for you

May your heart always be joyful
May your song always be sung
May you stay
Forever young

—Bob Dylan, "Forever Young"

My sister Ellen was only a year older than me, but even when we were adults, she tended to look out for me like a big sister. "Lighten up, Peter," she would kid when she was trying to encourage me to relax and take more time to have fun. Ellen often told me how proud she was that I had gone to medical school and become a doctor. She always gave me lots of approval and support, but she was concerned that I took life too seriously and that I didn't take enough time for myself.

Ellen was just the opposite. She had chosen to work as a waitress in Aspen, Colorado, so that she could have a full active outdoor lifestyle. She was a very beautiful woman, which seemed to be a prerequisite for the type of places where she worked. She loved meeting interesting people and had met and become friends with many of the celebrities who visited Aspen. I was so impressed when she told me she had served breakfast to both famed actor Clint Eastwood and world statesman Henry Kissinger at different tables on the same morning. She was very social and not one to turn down an invitation to a party or a night of dancing.

On one of my vacations, I arrived in the late evening at the restaurant where she worked. She introduced me to the

Eagles rock band. I retired to my room to rest from my journey, while she went out "flying with Eagles." She also loved adventure and was an avid climber and skier. I think she sometimes felt she should be doing something more professional like me. I know I often felt I should be living my life in a more immediate way like Ellen was.

Sometimes I pictured us in our sixties, sitting on a front porch, reminiscing about all the things we had done. She would tell me about the time she had led an all-woman climb in the Rocky Mountains or what celebrities had come to the restaurant where she worked. I would tell her about my experiences working in the emergency room or about the first time I delivered a baby and how nervous I was and how wonderful it all turned out to be.

I loved kidding Ellen and playing pranks because she was such a good sport and seemed to enjoy my pranks as much as I did. I was in England at the time she was planning her second marriage, and I had told her that I wouldn't be able to be back in time for the wedding. After thinking more about it, I decided that I really didn't want to miss it.

Without telling anyone, I flew directly from London to Aspen on the day before Ellen's wedding. I called her from the Aspen airport and pretended that I was still in England and that I was calling to congratulate her and tell her how much I was going to miss being there for the wedding. She told me that she really wished I could come to the wedding but that she understood why I couldn't. We talked about my ultramarathon race in England, where I had just completed my fifty-plus mile run from London to Brighton. The "plus" was the result of a number of detours on the road, and we were forced to run farther than the advertised fifty miles. Ellen elaborated on the details of her wedding plans.

During our conversation Ellen kept commenting on how good the phone connection was for a long-distance call, and I kept agreeing. Finally, I couldn't take it anymore. I told her that I was at the Aspen airport and needed a ride. When she picked me up fifteen minutes later, she was still crying and laughing all at once.

Forever Young

The wedding was beautiful. The ceremony took place on a warm fall afternoon in a meadow filled with wildflowers and surrounded by mountains. Yellow aspen leaves rustled in a soft breeze. A friend flew by the proceedings in a glider to wish Ellen and her husband-to-be, Michael, a happy life together. Ellen had a garland of wildflowers in her hair. She was so beautiful.

From Ellen and Michael's wedding invitation, 1979

That is the way I remember her best. Eight months after her wedding, she and Michael were killed when two small planes collided over Aspen on June 18, 1980. Ten people were killed in the crash, all of them friends or acquaintances. When my father called to tell me, I was stunned. How could this be happening again to me, to my family? I tried to make some sense of it, but I couldn't. First Charlotte, and now Ellen. I had no sisters left. I was devastated. I clung to my new girlfriend, Karen, and cried in her arms. "Don't leave me," I sobbed, "please don't leave me."

Karen and I flew to Aspen to be with my family and the other families for the funeral services. Aspen was still a relatively small town in 1980, and the whole community was grieving the loss of these family members and friends.

Probably as a result of my experience with Charlotte's death eleven years earlier, I came to an initial acceptance of Ellen's death within a relatively short time. There was a steady stream of friends and relatives coming to Ellen's and Michael's house where we stayed to talk about the loss. I felt centered and strong enough to support and share with those who were unaccepting or angry over Ellen's and Michael's deaths.

As I shared with people about Ellen and what a wonderful person she was and how much she was loved and missed, I realized that I was continuing to experience her life even though she was gone. Through this sharing with her friends, I was able to go on expeditions with her and watch her work at the restaurant and do things with her that I hadn't done with her when she was alive. I revisited my own memories of her and felt tremendous joy in our relationship.

Ashes to Ashes

The families of those who had been killed held a joint memorial service in Aspen, and it seemed that the entire community attended. During the service friends and family members were given time to stand and share their feelings. Several young children stood and said how much they were going to miss their mommy and daddy. It hurt to think how hard it would be for adults to get over the loss of these loved ones, and I wondered if that would even be possible for these children.

Our family and Michael's family scattered Ellen's and Michael's ashes in an aspen grove near the Maroon Bells, three rounded peaks that jut up above a beautiful alpine valley. I had hiked the Maroon Bells with Ellen, and I had wonderful memories of those trips. I loved being there and reliving those memories. I thought back to the memorial service when one of Ellen's friends had said that he felt Ellen was probably looking down on us saying, as she often used to say, "Lighten up, guys." She was so full of life that she would have rebelled at so much hurt and pain on her account. I could feel Ellen's presence there in the aspen grove when we scattered her ashes. She was looking down at us laughing and saying, "Why are you so upset? I'm happy and safe. Be happy with me."

At the memorial service Ellen's first husband, Jerry, sang "Forever Young," a song written by Bob Dylan. I think of that song now as a very beautiful prayer. Even as I age and change, I still think of Ellen as she was then—mischievous, laughing, forever young.

Living in the Present

After Ellen's death I could no longer rely on her to provide that sense of adventure and excitement that I had experienced vicariously through her. It was now up to me to do that for myself. She had always lived life to the fullest as if there was never any good reason to put off excitement and fun until another day. That is what I learned most powerfully from her death, that life is meant to be lived to its fullest at each moment.

When Charlotte died, I came to that same realization, and I had in many ways lived my life more in the present. But to a great extent I had let my concerns over my professional success crowd out my commitment to being full of life each day.

The commitment to live each day fully is something that often gets lost in the routine. Worries about the future can preoccupy us unnecessarily and sap tremendous energy. Sometimes when thoughts about dying prematurely from diabetes entered my mind, I would think about my sisters and realize that life is unpredictable, and we have no guarantees. It made me appreciate the life I had.

To ensure that I didn't slip back from this awareness and commitment, I learned to ask myself two questions each day:

> "What can I do today for myself that will make me feel good today about living?"
>
> "What would I most like to do with this day?"

The Good Son

Of all the members of my family, my mother seemed to take Ellen's death the hardest. She had been devastated by Charlotte's death, and it had taken years for her to get over that loss. Ellen's death seemed to put her right back where she had been. I spent a week with her and our long-time family friend, Mary, taking care of Ellen's estate. We went through Ellen's possessions, packed some of them to send to family members, and disposed of others.

As it turned out, that week was an extremely difficult experience for me. I wanted to expedite handling Ellen's affairs and to pass on or dispose of her belongings in the most efficient manner. I wanted to finish our work and move on to other things. To me it seemed that Mother wanted to spend time reminiscing and grieving. I felt that the process dragged on unnecessarily.

I remember being particularly frustrated at one point when Mother actually wanted to save some of Ellen's rags because they had sentimental value for her. I didn't come right out and say so, but I thought this was ridiculous. I was completely put out with Mother and was having a very hard time accepting anything she did. Somehow Mary got us both through the process. I left at the end of the week feeling tremendous strain, stress, and frustration.

I later realized that I stayed to help Mother because I knew how hard she was taking everything, and I felt that as a good son I should stay and support her. I made the choice to stay and help her for the wrong reasons. I wanted to see myself as a good son. If I couldn't take care of my own mother during her time of loss, then how could I tell myself that I was the person I was supposed to be? I was trying to fix my mother's problems so that I could tell myself I was a good person. I wasn't really taking care of my mother's needs or my own.

My mother needed to grieve the loss she felt at Ellen's death. I wanted to be out hiking and skiing with Ellen's friends and celebrating the life she had lived. Instead of meeting my own needs, I chose to play the role of the person I thought I should be. And I did a poor job at that. I wasn't really sensitive to my mother's needs and simply increased the strain on her. In the end neither of us got what we needed.

I've learned since then that if someone is in a certain frame of mind, that is his or her choice, and it may be the best choice given all the circumstances. This has led me to be more accepting of whatever choice a person has made because I realized that it wasn't necessary for me to intervene and rescue others from their choices. In fact, it was quite the opposite. Accepting someone's choice showed that person that I trusted their judgment and their ability to heal themselves.

I do not believe that we can ever truly help another person when our primary intent is to reassure ourselves that we are good people. We can pretend that we are helping someone else, but what we give under false pretenses is rarely beneficial. To understand what another person really wants or needs, one has to really listen. If we have our own needs to attend to, this diverts our attention. I do not believe that taking care of one's own needs is selfish or negative. Often only after we have first attended to our own needs, are we in a position to be truly helpful.

6

The Black Flag

Everything is miraculous. It is miraculous that one does not melt in one's bath.
—Picasso

I had come to love Kentucky during my residency there and wanted to stay and set up a medical practice. Two friends from residency and I started looking for a county that needed help. With our medical knowledge and newly acquired credentials, we felt we could really do some good. Garrard, a county with some 11,000 people and only one other doctor, caught our attention. Its population was predominantly elderly, its economy rural and depressed, its medical needs largely unmet. It was perfect.

We set up practice in an old log building in Lancaster, Kentucky in early 1980 and went about trying to solve Garrard County's medical problems with missionary zeal. In the clinic we got a frontline, in-the-trenches experience that would never have been possible in a larger town. We did almost everything. One night, for example, I spent three hours reattaching the scalp of a farmer who'd been thrown from a horse. On another night, the county ambulance volunteers brought in a 70-year-old man whose heart had stopped. We laid him on the emergency room stretcher and went to work on him, performing CPR and applying shocks to revive his heart.

Moments later he opened his eyes. He sat up. "What happened?" he asked, "and where's my wife?"

"I'll go get her," I told him.

Five minutes previously he had been dead. Now he was alive. I felt as if I were talking to a ghost. It was amazing to feel that we held life and death in our hands.

Life was so hard and poverty so widespread that people usually couldn't get medical treatment elsewhere. We only charged what we thought people could afford, which wasn't much. Our payment was largely the esteem in which we were held by those we helped. People were warm and appreciative and would find ways to be helpful. When my car needed repairs, my bill reflected only the cost of parts. It was a wonderful feeling to be doing so much good, to feel so appreciated and needed everywhere I went.

But such esteem had its price. We found ourselves regularly working 85-hour weeks, and eventually my excitement began to give way to exhaustion. I would work for long stretches with little sleep and tremendous stress.

One night while I was in surgery, repairing the arm of a man who'd gotten entangled in his tractor, I was informed that I was needed to make a delivery. I took off my surgical gloves, rushed to another room, put on new gloves, delivered the baby, rushed back to the mangled arm, put on new gloves, picked up the pieces, and started sewing again.

Such juggling of medical emergencies was not unusual. Even at home, it was impossible to relax. I lived only five minutes from the emergency room and would get calls at all hours of the night. Vacations were hard to come by.

An Unhealthy Pace

I continued to run and to spend time with my girlfriend, Karen, but there seemed to be little else in my life except work and the occasional race. I was constantly on edge, and deep down I was upset that I never had time for myself.

The long tiring weeks at work stretched into months and then into years. One Christmas, I made special arrangements not to be on call so that I could spend time with my parents. During Christmas dinner the phone rang. I was needed to deliver a baby. I delivered the baby and was getting ready to go home when someone else came in needing stitches. My parents had Christmas dinner without me at my house.

My family warned me that I had to slow down. I knew my pace wasn't healthy, but I now had obligations to the bank that had financed our practice, and I had a routine going. People expected things of me. I felt I couldn't say no.

One day in September 1982, I was out on a run and noticed a wavy black flag blocking part of the field of vision in my right eye. In the space of one hour the dark blot spread until I had completely lost vision in the eye. I immediately went to see my eye doctor. The black flag, he said, was a hemorrhage, my first evidence of diabetic eye disease.

Deep inside I knew the meaning of the black flag. I remembered the picture of the blind man with the white cane that I had seen at age fourteen, when I was first being educated about the effects of diabetes. I thought back to my medical school training.

Running a race in Kentucky with my friend Joni. The can of soda in my hand was in case I needed sugar during the race.

Open My Eyes: A Doctor's Powerful Story of Courage & Healing

Diabetic eye disease is the body's response to a lack of blood flow to the retina. The oxygen-starved retina produces fragile new blood vessels, which break and bleed easily. These hemorrhages may be small enough that the eye can reabsorb them, or they may be severe. The growth of new blood cells may also cause the retina, the screen in the eye on which the outer world is captured, to detach from the back of the eye. Permanent blindness can result from either hemorrhaging or retinal detachment.

My eye doctor and I discussed my options, which were few. When I asked him if anything could be done about clearing the blood from my right eye, he said we would just have to wait and see. I decided to follow the accepted practice at the time, to wait and see if the hemorrhage would clear on its own.

I knew that the deterioration of my eye was related to stress. I could not keep working at the pace I had set. I was blinding myself. I talked to my medical partners about making changes, lightening my load. But the stresses of my decade-long struggle to establish myself as a doctor had already taken a toll.

As I waited for my right eye to clear, my left eye began to show signs of deterioration. The anxiety I had felt about my hemorrhage, which I had viewed as an isolated problem, turned to fear. A trend was now evident. The disease was progressing.

My eye doctor recommended laser photocoagulation therapy to halt the deterioration of my left eye. In this therapy a laser is used to burn and scar the blood vessels that go to the edge of the eye with the goal of directing the blood flow to the center of the eye, thus preserving some vision. The laser destroys the peripheral vision so as to preserve the central vision. At risk of losing my vision altogether, I accepted my doctor's recommendation and agreed to the laser treatments.

I started laser treatment on my good eye—the one I could still see out of—within a couple of weeks after the hemorrhage that had blinded my right eye. The months of laser treatments were painful and frightening. I was thirty-two years old, and my nerve endings were still fully functional. I would press my head against the examining room wall so I couldn't jerk back when the doctor stuck a two-inch needle straight in underneath my eye. The shot was supposed to numb the eye and help when the laser burned into it. Fortunately, today's laser treatments feature numbing drops, not needles.

It was so painful, I nearly blacked out. Next, my chin and forehead were strapped against a bar and a slit lamp directed into my eyes. I was asked to keep my eyes wide open while the laser pinpointed its target. Each time the laser fired I could feel each excruciating flash. And if I blinked at the wrong time, the laser would burn a hole in the eyelid and hit the wrong place inside the eye.

For each treatment I would drive thirty-five miles, arrive at the appointed time, and then sit for hours in a waiting room with other frightened, uncomfortable, tired people. After the laser treatment, my seeing eye would swell so much that it was hard to see, and I would have to arrange for someone to pick me up and drive me home.

I was unsuccessful in lightening my load at work. It was simply impossible for four doctors to keep up with the needs of a whole county. We tried to send people to a nearby town for treatment, particularly if their needs could be better met by a specialist, but they were generally unwilling to go.

"You do it, Doc, or I won't have it done," one man told me after I'd recommended he go to Lexington for a complicated and risky surgery. I finally convinced him to go.

As often as not, people would refuse to see a specialist, and I would have to do the best job I could. As the strain increased, the only solution that seemed realistic to me was to leave Garrard County altogether.

I talked to my partners about selling my part of the business. They pointed out that this wouldn't be easy since the practice had no paper value, and we were all deeply in debt to the bank. Besides, they didn't want to continue in this practice without me. I felt trapped.

The hemorrhage in my right eye showed no sign of clearing. After eighteen months of waiting, my doctor and I finally made the decision that I would have a vitrectomy, a delicate and chancy surgery to try to restore vision in my right eye. The surgeon would cut open the globe, try to remove the bloody vitreous gel and scar tissue attachments without causing additional bleeding or dislodging the lens of the eye, and then refill the globe with a saline solution.

My eye doctor suggested I stop running because he was afraid that running might jar my left eye and cause more bleeding. I would do whatever it took to save my eyes, so I stopped running for the first time since high school. I started to gain weight and to feel lethargic. I had trouble keeping my blood sugar normal. I felt constantly anxious.

The Need to Be Needed

I was confused and depressed. How had I come to this? How was it that after struggling so hard to help, to become a doctor, to overcome obstacles and to be a good model of health and optimism, how had I ended up so ill, so entangled, and so anxious?

At the time I left my residency program—before starting my practice—I was feeling angry and burned out from the physical and emotional trauma of regular, round-the-clock shifts at our seriously understaffed hospital. What astonishes me now is that while I was still feeling angry and burned out, I chose to start a practice in one of the counties in Kentucky most desperately in need of medical services. Why did I put myself right back into such an unhealthy situation? I see now that I had a great need to be needed.

I had learned to use helping as a way to get approval, to feel good about myself. As I slowly burned myself out, I was operating on the belief I was only good if I was helping, in my case helping as a doctor. This is a very destructive belief. A newborn infant does not have to do anything to be lovable. A baby is worthy of love simply by the miracle of its existence. We are all deserving of that love simply because we are part of that same miracle. Yet, as children we learn that society gives or withholds approval based on what we do or achieve or produce. To society we may have no inherent value. This training is, I believe, the foundation for many illnesses.

I link the extent of my eye damage directly to the stress and strain I chose as a young medical student and doctor. And I believe I chose that stress and strain because I didn't fully value myself. I had learned to value myself through the eyes of society, not through an inner sense of myself.

The helplessness I had experienced at the time of the crash that injured Kenny and killed Charlotte had been transformed into a real desire to help others. Now that desire had progressed to an unhealthy extreme. I was very dependent on my doctor/helper role for my feelings of self-worth.

When we try to help others, we sometimes act out of natural compassion, out of that deep well of goodness that is at our very center. In those moments we are outside ourselves, tuning into the needs of others, really helping. At other times, we act out of a need to see ourselves as helpers, as "good." In these moments we are acting out a role, and we are really focused on our own needs more than the needs of the person we're pretending to help. We may not actually be helping at all because we're not really tuning in to what's needed.

When I find myself getting lost in the helper role, I try to take a time-out. I try to get in touch with my conviction that I am a good person whether or not I'm helping, and that I like and care about myself. I remind myself that I don't need to play the part of the concerned doctor to feel good about myself. When I am grounded and feeling good about myself and my basic human goodness and my connection with other humans, I am in a better place to act out of natural compassion, to be truly helpful.

My relationships at the time, like my professional activities, were based partly on a lack of self-esteem. Karen said once that she would have liked to live in a little cabin in the woods with me and never see another person as long as she lived. At the time I viewed this as stifling and my girlfriend as being dependent. Later I realized that I was also dependent. I chose her as a partner partly because I was acting once again out of my need to be needed. Because I did not fully value myself, I needed someone to do it for me.

A Helping Hand

As I struggled to come to terms with my deteriorating eyesight, I found a new source of strength and hope, the American Society of Handicapped Physicians (ASHP). This was an organization of physicians with disabilities of all types—some paralyzed by accidents, some with degenerative diseases, others who had lost sight or hearing.

In May 1984 I attended a meeting of the ASHP and felt immediately at home in this association. It was a community where the members grew through genuine giving and receiving.

This society had been founded in 1981 by Dr. Spencer B. Lewis, a family practice doctor who, like me, had diabetes with progressive retinopathy. Within a few years the society had grown to over 800 members in forty-six states. Although the ASHP no longer exists, the support and resources it provided then are now available from the Society for Healthcare Professionals with Disabilities, launched by Dr. Joseph Kim in 2010.

Through the ASHP I met several practicing physicians who were blind. Dr. Marla Bernbaum, who had diabetes and was blind, explained to me how she used a physician's assistant to do the visual part of her exams. I was also befriended by Dr. Stan Wainapel, a blind physician who became a source of support as my eyesight deteriorated. He would call or write from time to time just to find out how I was doing. His gentle compassion had such a healing influence that I began to realize that my own power as a healer resided perhaps more in my heart than in my eyes. What he was doing for me, I could do for others.

Through the association I saw examples of real bravery. One time at the ASHP national meeting, I met a physician I will call Jim, a slight, wiry man who suffered from frequent and severe epileptic seizures. Although Jim was a very intelligent man, his epilepsy was so disabling that he no longer practiced medicine. His wife Sally was a pediatrician and an officer in the association although she had no physical disabilities.

During one of the conference sessions, Jim suddenly emitted a loud growl. I turned to see his head lurch back and his body go rigid. As I turned to help, his body erupted into a grand mal seizure. Sally jumped reflexively from her chair to help him. She wrapped her arms around him and hugged him to prevent him from hurting himself. She held Jim through the whole seizure. After the seizure we moved him to the floor where he could sleep, and went on with the meeting.

Later, I learned that his seizures were so frequent that he suffered from loss of memory. Sally spent a good deal of her time taking photographs of everything that happened and logging events to fill in what Jim's brain could no longer retain. "This is Dr. Powers," she would say. "You met him last week, and this is what you did together . . . " They were both trying very hard.

As bad as my own experience was at times, I saw that it could be a lot worse. I felt lucky to have good mental function. I realized that self-pity really would not serve me very well. I felt tremendous admiration for this kind of love and bravery. I saw that it was possible to handle even the worst disabilities with dignity and courage.

7

An Atmosphere of Celebration

Change the way you look at things and the things you look at change.
—Wayne W. Dyer

I continued to try to make changes in my life to ease some of the accumulated stresses. I found a buyer for our Kentucky practice, someone who would step in and assume the debts. And I insisted on some time off. I did some traveling and some hiking. At about the time the sale of our medical practice was finalized, Karen and I broke up. I moved to nearby Berea, Kentucky, where there were more doctors, and I could work without so much pressure.

At one of the Farlander events at Weeona Lake, I met Beth, and soon after we were a couple. After putting up with the challenges of a long-distance relationship, she joined me in Berea. I also planned a vacation to visit my brother Kenny, who had moved to Alaska in 1980.

Kenny had done well in college, and after graduating from the University of Minnesota, he moved to the D.C. area and attended law school at Georgetown University. His first job as an attorney was working as a clerk for a federal judge in Anchorage defending conservation lands.

A trip to see Kenny, I felt, might help take my mind off my upcoming operation. I flew to Anchorage two weeks prior to my vitrectomy surgery.

Alaska was enchanting, especially for a stressed-out, rural doctor. We rafted the Tazlina River, a winding, bucking river that twisted through wilderness that seemed to stretch forever around us. As we explored vast forests where perhaps no one had ever walked before, and followed the sun across rugged, glacier-carved landscapes, I was struck by the contrast between this place and others. In Kentucky life seemed so hard; the focus was on just trying to get your work done. There was no celebrating. In Alaska it seemed there was a real zest for living, for doing things, particularly outdoor things.

I felt that an atmosphere of living and doing and celebrating would help me heal. Beth agreed, and we decided to move to Alaska as soon as I could make arrangements.

Being a Patient

First, however, there was surgery to attend to. In the spring of 1984, I flew directly to Boston for vitrectomy surgery on my right eye. My operation was scheduled at the Massachusetts Eye and Ear Institute, which housed some of the best surgeons in the country. I showed up for my first appointment full of anticipation—and ten minutes early.

Four long irritating hours later I was called in for a brief meeting with the surgeon who was to operate on me. No explanation for the wait was offered. I'd heard about places where the value of a patient's time was not respected, where a patient was treated as one of many unimportant supplicants, but I couldn't believe this had happened to me. I had been subjected to one of the most demeaning practices of my profession. With my confidence shaken by this experience, I entered the hospital to prepare for surgery.

My anesthesiologist gave me a brief, cursory exam the night before surgery. After taking a very superficial history and writing down the medications I was taking, he left. He didn't take the time to listen to my heart and lungs or even shake my hand. This was the man who was responsible for keeping me alive during the operation. As a physician, I felt this type of treatment was not just dehumanizing but also medically inadequate.

Fortunately, I was in good health, and I knew it. I felt empathy for patients who were not doctors and who would have no way of assuring themselves that they were getting the care that they needed.

Later that evening, a nurse came in to give me a shot of antibiotics. Since I already had an intravenous line going, I asked if she could give me the antibiotic intravenously. The nurse insisted on giving me a shot in the buttocks—those were the surgeon's orders. I knew that the order could just be rewritten and suggested this. But the nurse was insistent.

Wanting to be a good patient, I acquiesced. The antibiotic, once injected into the muscle, was so painful that the nurse had to help me walk for forty minutes before I could even consider sitting down again. Intravenously, it would have been painless.

The whole episode was unnecessary except as a lesson for me to be less worried about being a good patient and more assertive about getting my needs met. I was already concerned about the quality and the humaneness of the treatment I was receiving. The physical pain of the shot just added to my apprehension.

My surgery seemed to go well, although we wouldn't know for a couple of months if it had been successful. The day after surgery I was upset to discover that my blood sugar levels, which were being monitored by the hospital staff, were higher than they'd ever been. I was there for treatment of a health problem, and the regulation of my blood sugar, which was so essential to my good health, was being handled carelessly. I asked for, and received, an order that would allow me to administer my own insulin and be responsible for my own glucose monitoring.

If I had been trying to do too much in my role as helper, I was doing too little in my role as patient. The passive patient role is one that is built into the healthcare system. Why, for example, do we call an ill person a "patient?" The word implies waiting out something over which you have no control. Did we somewhere get the idea that an ill person should sit passively, "patiently," helplessly by and let someone else control his or her destiny? It describes the role some doctors want their clients to play, the role of supplicant. For these doctors the idea is "come pay me for my expertise, but don't question my authority and don't disturb my routine." Is "patient" a label some doctor came up with to try to get people to feel okay about sitting around for four hours in a waiting room?

My hospital experiences reaffirmed my conviction that a person should never give up his or her own power, even to healthcare professionals. A person goes to a doctor because the doctor is a specialist in helping others overcome illness. But helping involves cooperation and participation, not control. A person must be an active participant in his or her own healing. No one is more informed than the patient about the patient's body.

In this instance, no one in the hospital would be as conscientious as I would be in seeing that I stayed in good diabetic control. Yet, I had to challenge the hospital routine to get the healthcare professionals to let me assume that responsibility for myself.

Breaking Down Roles — Peter, the Unhelpful

My mother helped care for me during my convalescence at her home in Boston. In the weeks that followed my surgery, my eye showed signs of healing. Feeling some hope, I began to plan my move to Alaska. My mother suggested she could travel with me back to Kentucky and help me move. She knew that Beth was away visiting family and friends before our move to Alaska and wasn't available.

I felt that I didn't need my mother's help and told her I would be able to pack just fine. She was so persistent in her offer to help that I finally decided that even if her presence were a hindrance, I could put up with it.

I was wrong. The ten-day packing period was a nightmare. We quarreled over who was in charge of packing, what was the proper way to pack, and even what should be packed. I was particularly distressed that Mother would often insist on sitting and talking in the middle of packing sessions. She was trying, indirectly, as she later told me, to deal with her own terror and sense of loss over my blindness.

For my part, I had my hands full dealing not only with my deteriorating health and recovery from surgery, but also with leaving my friends and a place that I loved, not to mention the security of my job. Emotionally, neither my mother nor I were in a place to be helpful to the other. Yet we continued with the avowed intention of getting my things packed in time for me to get to a friend's wedding in Alaska.

After ten days the boxes were mislabeled, and everything was in total confusion. My mother's plan was now to fly to Alaska with me where we would extend this ordeal another two weeks. I finally broke down.

"This is not helpful to me," I burst out in the middle of one argument. "I can't stand this anymore, and you are not welcome to come to Alaska with me."

I left for Alaska feeling confused, upset, and guilty about the interaction with my mother. Helping was supposed to be my specialty, and yet, I felt I had failed miserably in my efforts to help her.

Years later in thinking back on this situation, I understood more about the interaction with my mother. When she insisted on helping me pack, I could see that she was focused on her own needs and that her "help" would not really be helpful to me. My mistake was to counter her helper role with a helper role of my own. I decided to "help" her by letting her help me pack. Role-playing got us nowhere, and neither of us got our needs met.

What I had perceived as a failing on my part—telling my mother that she was not welcome to come to Alaska with me—may have been the healthiest part of the whole interaction. I had let go of my act and said what I really felt. For a moment, I had accepted who I was. I was admitting that I was human and vulnerable and perhaps even unhelpful at times.

The first step toward rediscovering our natural goodness is to acknowledge who we are and accept ourselves as we are. Faced with the same choice today, I would try to be truly helpful to all concerned, and I would not slight my own needs in the process. I would look for a way to create a win-win situation.

Communication, creativity, and openness are the keys. When all else fails, I believe that we have a responsibility to help ourselves first. Only then are we even in a position to be of help to others.

Challenging the System

Settling into a small apartment in Anchorage with Beth in late spring 1984, I went right to work for a clinic that served low-income and indigent people. In July, I applied for hospital privileges and was surprised to find that one of the two local hospitals denied my application. I was informed that my visual impairment made me unfit to practice medicine in their hospital.

I was stunned by their ignorance and prejudice and was eager to confront them. Angered, I scheduled a meeting with the hospital appeals board. I produced letters of recommendation from former colleagues and from friends in the American Society of Handicapped Physicians. I presented statistics about the number of blind physicians in practice around the country. And I made a cogent argument that I was no less fit to practice than any of those who were reviewing me.

The board was convinced, but they didn't have the power to approve my hospital privileges. Next I would have to present my case to the hospital credentials committee. At this meeting, one doctor questioned my ability to read an x-ray or a cardiogram with my 20/200 vision.

I could read it, I said, even with my visual impairment. But I also pointed out that many doctors never read x-rays and cardiograms. They leave this to radiologists and cardiologists. And, I pointed out that none of their doctors, nor any other doctor in the country, had ever been required to read an x-ray to be granted hospital privileges. Their poorly thought-out reactions and objections didn't hold up under scrutiny.

The committee finally approved my hospital privileges, along with a grudging, and probably illegal, stipulation that my privileges be subject to a yearly visual exam. I had to wonder if the doctors who attempted to deny me hospital privileges felt in some fashion that being "able-bodied" put them on a higher plane than other people, and that admitting a "handicapped" person into their midst threatened their image of themselves. If a disabled person could do their job, it might seem less special.

Eventually, I became president of the American Society of Handicapped Physicians and presided over the national meetings during my two-year term.

Reaching Out

My right eye continued to heal, and by September, about three months after my move to Alaska, my vision was starting to clear. The surgery appeared to have been successful, and I felt hopeful.

Within the month, my left eye hemorrhaged. Upon examination, my eye doctor discovered that the retina had detached. Unless the retina could be reattached by emergency surgery, I would be permanently blind in my left eye. Numbed by continuous ups and downs, I was operating on automatic pilot, accepting each event, and just moving on to what needed to be done next. At least I could see out of my right eye now.

I prepared for the surgery, which could be performed in Anchorage. The clinic where I was working gave me a month off and assured me that my job would be waiting when I got back.

On my first postoperative day in the hospital, I was lying flat on my stomach with both eyes bandaged when a nurse came in to check my blood sugar. My eye doctor had put an air baffle in my left eye that was helping to hold the retina in place, so I had to remain positioned on the bed face down to keep the air baffle in place.

The nurse lanced my finger several times, getting a fresh blood sample each time, but couldn't seem to complete the glucose test. She said the machine kept reporting that there was an error; she was obviously struggling.

I finally asked if I could help, even though my eyes were completely covered by the bandages. As she handed me the machine and the bottle holding the chemistry strips, I realized by the feel of the small fat bottle that it didn't contain the right kind of strips.

"What does it say on this bottle?" I asked her.

"Keto-Diastix," she responded, not realizing that she had been using urine testing strips instead of blood test strips.

"Yikes," I thought, "and this nurse is drawing up my insulin dose!"

The next day when the patches were off my eyes, I started doing my own glucose monitoring again.

For about a week it appeared that the operation had been successful. Then the doctor discovered that the retina had not reattached. There was no longer a connection by which it could capture images of the outside world. I would never see out of my left eye again.

I reacted to the permanent blindness in my left eye with quiet resignation. "Well, I have two eyes," I thought. "I don't have to be able to see out of both of them." I didn't dwell on it. It was not bravery so much, perhaps, as distraction. I was in great pain, presumably from the operation. Then my doctor informed me that the pain was being caused by glaucoma, and that if the pain continued, the left eye might have to be totally removed.

Blindness seemed like a small thing next to the constant pain. But I was unnerved by the prospect of more surgery, more expense, and the thought of having a glass eye, which would always stare disconcertingly in one direction.

It seemed I was paying and paying and paying for the cumulative stresses of my medical apprenticeship. Maybe I wasn't making the right kinds of changes. Maybe I was still lost in my role as a helper. I was being hit again and again with the reality that Peter, the helper, needed help.

First and foremost, I needed my own help to learn to value and take care of myself. Secondly, I needed the help of other people to heal physically and emotionally.

Home alone in our apartment the week after the operation while Beth worked her nursing shift, I was recuperating, sitting at the dining room table, when the room began slowly getting darker—it went from a light haze, to smoke gray, to total blackness. It took about ten minutes, and there was no doubt in my mind about what was happening. My right eye was hemorrhaging again, the eye that I thought had healed. I sat at the table and cried.

I was now totally blind.

8

Dancing Blind

> *When you walk to the edge of all the light you have and take that first step into the darkness of the unknown, you must believe that one of two things will happen: There will be something solid for you to stand upon, or, you will be taught how to fly.*
> —Patrick Overton, "Faith"

As I sat alone in the darkness, I flashed on the picture of the blind beggar with cup and cane that I'd seen as a teenager in the brochures on diabetes. A lump that wouldn't go away with swallowing formed in my throat. What would I do? I didn't know how to be blind. I didn't want to be blind. I wanted my eyesight back. I wanted the life back that I knew and loved.

I had done everything I could to stop the blindness. All for nothing. I felt completely defeated, totally overwhelmed, and helpless.

I sat for a long time and cried.

Finally, a disconcerting memory confronted me. I had made plans to have dinner that evening with Mike, an old running friend from high school who was in town for a convention. I hadn't seen him since the day of his wedding, twelve years before. Now what was I going to do? How could I go out to dinner after just having gone blind? How could I make small talk? How could I eat? At first, I thought it best just to cancel dinner.

Then I began to think about the image that I had always held of myself. I was the one who was strong in hard times, the oldest son in a strong family. Surely I could handle dinner. After all, this was only blindness. I needed to hold things together—for myself and for everyone else. Embracing this image of myself, I got up from the table and began to explore my surroundings. I could find my way around the apartment. I could find things in my drawers. I could shower.

I was mostly ready to go when my brother Kenny came to pick me up. I was feeling like I might be all right, but as soon as he walked through the door, I started to cry again. By the time we arrived at the restaurant, I had assumed my old "chin-up" attitude and was even making jokes about which one of them would be my seeing-eye dog. Emotionally, though, I was a house of cards, ready to collapse.

As we walked in, I heard Kenny say, "Here's Mike now." He called out a greeting, and I heard Mike's voice answer. Then it hit me that I hadn't seen Mike in twelve years, and I still couldn't see him. The pain of having lost my vision overwhelmed me once again, my strongman routine caved in, and I broke down and cried.

Kenny was as unskilled at leading a blind person as I was at walking blind. He was hesitant to say or do something that would upset me, and so I banged into chairs all the way across the restaurant. A sixth sense told me that necks were craning, and eyes all around the restaurant were fixed on me.

When we ate dinner, I didn't know how to find my food without using my fingers. As I tried to pin my steak down and cut it, I knocked it off the plate and into my lap. Mike offered to cut it for me. I stabbed randomly around the plate trying to find the meat, and ended up with a big, terrible-tasting piece of fat in my mouth. I felt embarrassed and, at the same time, sheepish for being embarrassed. Mike was not taking any of this too seriously. In fact, he was jovial. Whatever I was seemed okay with him—blind or sighted, strong or weak. He was just happy to be with me again. I didn't have to pretend to be strong or helpful or anything else. I went home that night feeling better.

"Blind" School

Later that week, still on leave from work, I enrolled in the Alaska School for the Blind and Deaf in Anchorage. There I would learn how to cook, walk with a cane, read braille, and otherwise adjust to life as a blind person. While I accepted "blind" school wholeheartedly, I did not accept blindness. I knew that both of my surgeries seemed to have failed. I knew that traditional medicine had no more solutions. But I planned on seeing again. I just didn't know how. I was not denying the reality that I was blind, but I was determined not to surrender my own power to determine my future.

A short time after I started blind school, Beth and I found ourselves having more and more trouble getting along. We weren't happy anymore. Neither of us knew what was wrong. We talked about splitting up, but she was afraid our friends would think she was breaking up with me because of my blindness. I didn't know what to do about her concern except to reassure her that I didn't think that was the reason.

Eventually we did split up, and I moved in with Kenny. Beth later told me that it was my "helpfulness" that had driven her out of the relationship. She didn't need help; she needed to develop confidence in her own abilities.

Learning to walk blind was one of the most frightening experiences of my life. As we practiced with our canes, our instructors would let us walk into walls. They just tried to make sure we didn't do it too hard.

Every step was into the unknown, every misstep—as I stumbled off curbs or into signs—an exercise in controlling panic. Every car I heard sounded as if it were coming straight at me. Every person who gunned the engine and burned rubber threw me into a kind of terror.

The bus that took me home each day was about a half mile away from the school, down two busy streets. After I had learned basic walking skills, I learned how to find the bus stop on my own. I was taught to gauge my approach to the bus stop by how long I had been walking, rather than by counting steps. When I thought I was close to the stop, I would probe with my cane to find the sign itself. Eventually, I would hear the sound of a bus, doors would open in front of me, and I would get on. I had an initial hesitancy to ask the bus driver for help, which I overcame after getting on the wrong bus a couple of times. Each day as I walked to the stop, I was gripped with the fear that I might miss the curb with my cane, step off it, and pitch headlong into traffic.

Getting off the bus, I would always ask the driver to let me off at the stop before the railroad tracks in the neighborhood where Kenny and I lived. One day the driver dropped me off at the stop after the railroad tracks by mistake. Exiting the bus, I found myself on strange ground and with no familiar landmarks. Trying to find my way, I banged my head into a sign that jutted out from a building at head level. The pain was intense, but my frustration was worse.

I stood there feeling angry. "Why is this happening to me?" I asked silently. "I don't want to be blind. I didn't choose this." Eventually, I heard someone passing by and called out to ask where I was. When I was oriented, I started out again and slowly made my way home. Finding my way around was not so hard. The real struggle for me was the emotional reality that I could not take the blindfold off.

Braille was also a struggle. In part this may have been because of numbness in the tips of my fingers, a result of long-term diabetes. Perhaps it was also because I expected too much from myself. But most probably it was because I didn't believe I would ever need braille. I was insisting to myself that I would not always be blind.

Cooking class taught me all the things I should have known at the restaurant—how to handle knives and hot food. The instructors insisted that I learn how to boil and pour my own coffee in the first few days. Before long they also helped me work out a system for doing my own insulin injections.

Improving My Signature

In the first week of blind school, I went to the Social Security office in Anchorage with my travel trainer, Pam. She could use any unfamiliar building as a classroom for travel training, and I needed to apply for disability income to pay for my classes.

The interview was undertaken with a Social Security officer, a mature woman who sounded like she could be fifty or sixty years old. After about an hour of answering questions, it was time for me to sign about twenty different official papers to complete my application.

Unfortunately, I had no experience in trying to sign a document I couldn't see. Fortunately, Pam was very helpful and showed me how to sign by placing my left index finger exactly where the "X" might indicate for me to sign. I could then write my name in the general area calling for my signature.

Ironically, while doctors are notorious for their illegible handwriting, I had aways been the exception to that rule. Now I had an excuse to scribble my name, but it wouldn't have been recognizable as my signature. I wondered how I was doing, and whether anything I was signing would be legible. This was my first experience trying to write or sign anything since I had gone blind.

After several attempts, I finally asked for feedback from Pam about my signature. I queried, "Is there anything I need to do to make it better?"

My service-minded instructor promptly answered, "You could stretch out your Peter a little."

I was shocked and humored by her answer but didn't dare let it show since I couldn't see if Pam or the Social Security officer had recognized the inadvertent double meaning. I would have loved to have seen the twinkle in her eye, a flinch, or any sign of blushing. I didn't hear a sound from either woman in the pregnant pause that followed.

Eventually, I said, "Okay, thanks." I wanted to make a smart remark like, "Do you have any suggestions as to how I might do that?" But I had to content myself with simply stretching out the signature of my first name.

"Attitudes" Class

An "attitudes" class was also required for all of us enrolled in the school. The instructors talked to us about maintaining our self-esteem and realizing we were just as good and worthy as those who weren't blind, and that we could be happy and productive.

This class proved to be a painful reality for many students, and our discussions would often bog down in silence. One girl was near tears every time she spoke. She had gone blind suddenly from glaucoma in the midst of university schooling. She couldn't even relate to discussions about how blind people can work as well as anyone else, she told us, because she had no work skills.

Another girl came from a wealthy family and seemed to feel that she didn't need special schooling at all because she was going to be taken care of. Others sat in silence, bottling up their feelings rather than exploring them.

One day in attitudes class we were working around the circle, and it wasn't even my turn to talk, but suddenly I was overcome with the urge, and I leapt up from my chair and shouted, "I refuse to be blind!"

The whole room went quiet. I had shocked myself and everyone else. I didn't even know where my outburst had come from, but I felt a shift deep inside me. Spirit moved in me at that moment. I felt like I had been struck by lightning. Perhaps I had been struck by a Light.

From that moment, I knew I would not remain blind.

I was a big contributor to these discussions, but mostly out of goodwill, because I felt I already understood the topic well. I had been living with diabetes for twenty years since childhood and had been fighting the loss of my vision for some time. I knew about accepting losses and keeping a good attitude. And besides, I felt I wasn't really going to stay blind. I felt like I'd rather be out practicing with my cane so I could get by in the short term.

Fortunately for me, the staff didn't buy this. They made it clear that they valued my insights and experience and felt I was important to the success of the class. I felt a lot of love from them. I think they also recognized I needed to be in the attitudes class because I had more to learn.

And, indeed, the lessons were ones I would find very helpful. Among other things, I was learning—perhaps for the first time—to value myself, help myself, and care for myself. Spending so much time exclusively devoted to myself was a new experience. But none of this took the fear or frustration out of walking blind. I'd later tell friends that, all in all, school for the blind was a tremendous learning and growing experience—and one that I wouldn't recommend to anybody.

Obstacles and Opportunities

During my time off from work, I'd updated my employer on my recovery from eye surgery. A week before I was supposed to be back at my job at the Anchorage Neighborhood Health Center, I called to let them know that I'd been bleeding in my good eye and that I'd need an extra week or so off. Their response was that business was slow, and they probably didn't need me to come back at all.

When I called to check in with them a week later, they flatly told me they'd eliminated my position, and that I no longer had a job. Apparently, they thought I couldn't be effective as a blind doctor and were hoping I'd just go away.

Three weeks after telling me they didn't have enough work to keep me busy, they filled my position with a new doctor, someone I knew. I felt deeply wronged. It appeared that the clinic directors were ignorant as to how blindness would affect my ability to treat people, and they were simply unwilling to take the time and energy to learn about it.

I also knew that what they had done was illegal. In the decade since my experience with medical school admission, federal laws had been passed prohibiting discrimination on the basis of a disability. I thought about filing a lawsuit to make a point—to save others with disabilities from that kind of prejudice—but I had conflicting concerns. The clinic was one of the few places that cared for the city's poor. If I sued and won, the government might withdraw the clinic's funding, and that would harm the indigent people of the city. I was torn. There seemed to be no good solution.

I finally decided that even if the clinic showed a lack of judgment in my circumstance, they did provide a service to the community, and I would not get in the way of that service. It was not a satisfying resolution, but I felt I had to set the question aside and move on with my life.

I started scouting around to see what other places in town might need a doctor. I would call directory assistance to get the number of a medical clinic or family practice. Then I would call the clinic or practice to find out if they needed help. I would tell them I was new in town and that I had worked for a couple of months at a place that was overstaffed. I had taken some time off for a vision problem, I said, and now I was ready to go back to work and was checking out job possibilities.

I was careful not to set myself up for rejection by asking for anything. I was only exploring possibilities at this point. It was the first time I'd ever had to job hunt. Before this, my only concern had been how to choose between many opportunities.

Realizing that my anger about losing my job with the clinic would only hurt me, I began to focus my energy on showing what was right with me rather than what was wrong with the clinic. I would put my best foot forward in spite of my blindness, in spite of the discrimination of others. The clinic's loss would be someone else's gain.

Paradoxically, the loss of my job was setting in motion a process in which I was beginning to gain self-esteem. And thereby, I was learning an important lesson. I was learning to look at loss and see in it an opportunity. I began trying to make a conscious habit of looking at all obstacles and defeats as opportunities for growth and change. When my hopes and expectations were defeated, I began looking for the new possibilities inherent in the situation.

Initially, this seemed to be the only way to salvage my feelings over my blindness, the loss of my job, the loss of my relationship, and the social isolation. It seemed the only way to feel optimism or hope instead of despair. Gradually, I began to understand what a powerful tool this could be for dealing with any struggle.

After a few weeks, I hadn't turned up any real job opportunities. As I tried to find a positive way to interpret what was happening, I realized that I didn't have to be rushing around so much. Maybe I could just ease off a bit and wait for the right opportunity to come up. I didn't have to be working or helping others to be worthwhile. I was worthwhile just by virtue of the fact that I existed.

I thought back to the attitudes class and realized this is what they had been trying to teach me in those discussions where I was so sure I already understood everything. Now I felt support coming from inside. My own support was nurturing. I felt gratitude toward my instructors.

Being a Friend

As I tried to adjust socially to blindness, a sense of isolation and dependency dogged me. When I went to parties, I couldn't talk with people freely because I didn't know who was there. And even if I knew people there, I wouldn't be able to find them without help. Sitting and waiting for people to come talk to me, I'd get a sinking feeling.

I relied a lot on Kenny and other friends for transportation. As helpful as Kenny and others were, I knew that they had their own lives to live, and I struggled with the feeling that I was a burden. Increasingly, I felt very hopeless.

One evening at a party Kenny was hosting at our house, I was sitting on the couch listening to the chatter and laughter around me when a friend of Kenny's came up and introduced himself. He knew I was a doctor. He told me he'd been having stomach pain and digestive problems for several years. Unable to find any medical problem, his doctors had referred him for psychiatric help. Because of the implication that he had psychological problems, his health insurer limited and then denied his coverage. This had shaken his confidence both in the medical profession and his own sense of security. His condition had been recently diagnosed as a legitimate medical problem, but he didn't know how much he should trust what he was now being told.

Having been a patient myself and having learned how arrogant doctors can be at times, particularly when they don't know what is wrong with a person, I sympathized. I told him that I didn't accept my doctor's advice as anything more than an educated opinion, and I didn't think he should, either.

I told him there's always the possibility of further healing, and that there was nothing wrong with him that could not be healed. I was fervent about my belief that we could heal anything that was wrong with us because I was dealing with the same issue. I was saying things that came from deep inside, things that I needed to say to myself, things that I wanted very much to prove true for myself.

He said that his doctor had told him to stop his exercise program because it aggravated his symptoms.

I said, "Yes, I can understand why a doctor might say that, but you don't have to follow that advice because I don't believe it's accurate in your case. I'm sure you can find a way to exercise that won't aggravate your symptoms."

I told him that if he would take charge of healing his own illness and follow his intuition, there was no reason to expect that he couldn't have a complete recovery and resume a normal life and a normal diet.

We talked for a long time, and I sensed that we connected. I felt tremendously encouraged as I realized how helpful I could be even though I was blind, even if I never worked as a doctor again. If nothing else, I could be a good friend.

Affirmations and Visualization

About this time, I heard that cancer treatment centers were having some success bringing cancers into partial or complete remission using a technique called visualization. I hired a friend to find a book on visualization and read it to me. In these sessions, I learned that visualization focused on using the power of the mind to heal the body. By simply imagining the healing process to be taking place, the author argued, a person could activate the body's healing mechanisms.

Although visualization had only limited acceptance in the medical community at that time, and many people thought of it as junk science, the author cited several studies that indicated a greater than average rate of recovery among people with terminal cancer who had followed a program of daily imaging exercises.

Today it is common for visualization techniques such as guided imagery to be used to help achieve a goal. For example, many ski athletes can be seen closing their eyes at the starting gate, performing a successful race in their minds so that their body can follow that winning program. From relaxation to healing to physical mastery, using imagination to form experiences in the mind can be powerful.

Evidence at the time also indicated that the more closely a person's visualization mirrored the body's actual healing process, the greater the likelihood the person would heal. I noted with interest that visualization appeared to be beneficial to a lesser degree even when it did not mirror the body's healing process. Perhaps this is because in either case the body recognizes the mind's willingness to heal.

Doubt itself, which is usually present to some degree, may decrease the likelihood of healing. The recognition of doubt as a factor in the healing process may be useful information for the ill person. Perhaps it means he or she doesn't really believe in the possibility of getting better. Perhaps it means the patient doesn't really believe he or she has any control over his or her life.

My eye surgeon had told me explicitly that there was nothing else that could be done for my blindness after the retinal detachment surgery failed to reattach the retina. Despite my years of medical training, I realized I needed to look to alternative methods for healing.

Although traditional medicine had no more answers for my blindness, it could provide me with a picture of the healing process, a model for visualization. I decided to try using visualization to clear the hemorrhage in my right eye. I made up my own exercise, creating a visualization that mimicked the process I thought my body might use to clear the hemorrhage.

First, I would sit and focus on my breathing until I was relaxed. Then I would breathe in deeply, and as I breathed in, I would visualize little white blood cells coming into the eye, each one like a little Pac-Man from the popular early video game.

In the game, the video player would move a round yellow character that resembled a hockey puck with an enormous mouth through an enclosed maze, gobbling up all the food-pellet dots while avoiding four colored ghosts. In my visualization exercise, each Pac-Man would eat up the red blood cells in my eye, the remnants of the hemorrhage.

Then, as I exhaled, all the little white blood cell Pac-Man characters, with their mouths full of red blood cells, would exit into my bloodstream, clearing the blood away from my eyes. I would do this visualization exercise continuously for ten to twenty minutes a day. The deep relaxation and the focus on taking care of myself felt rewarding.

I also began to talk to myself. "I will not be blind," I would tell myself. "I am regaining my sight. I am seeing better little by little."

This exercise, which I'd never heard of at the time, has come to be used widely in healing. These self-directed phrases are called "self-talk" or affirmations, and are an example of cognitive restructuring. The most important thing about these messages was that they felt true and right for me.

The theory behind cognitive restructuring is that a person's emotional well-being is the result of "messages" that run through his or her mind. These messages come from many sources—parents, society, religious training—and they may be conscious or unconscious. Many of them are so firmly embedded in our minds as children that we never question them. They are our "reality."

A state of depression or chronic guilt or anxiety might be the result of self-critical messages or beliefs that became ingrained in the person as a child, messages like "You're not good enough. You're fat, ugly, selfish, insensitive, irresponsible. . . You never think of other people. You are bad. You *should* feel bad."

We don't realize that although these thoughts can come to us unbidden, they do not represent an objective reality, and we do not have to be at their mercy. The process of changing these mental messages can create a healthier, less fearful environment for our emotions.

Many counseling techniques are aimed at helping people come up with new productive messages to counter the destructive messages that have become ingrained in their emotions. A common technique for dealing with depression is to have the depressed person write down a list of ten things he or she likes about him or herself and read this list aloud every day.

Another positive technique is to take a time-out to cycle good messages through our minds when we notice ourselves feeling "bad." Example messages to counter self-destructive emotions include:

"I am good and worthwhile exactly as I am."

"I am learning the lessons I need to learn."

"My existence is a miracle that is unfolding exactly as it should."

"I forgive myself for my tendency to judge myself harshly."

"I'm a caring, loving person."

"I love myself. I accept myself. I am my own best friend."

Studies indicate that a positive emotional state promotes healing. Cognitive restructuring can create an emotional climate for healing.

Resisting Isolation Through Dancing

The affirmations and visualizations helped emotionally, but I still felt isolated by my blindness. I continued trying to piece my social life back together. Before going blind I had been attending monthly dances with a local square dance group. Now I missed these dances. Ever since the barn dances my parents used to host at their farm in Illinois, I had enjoyed dancing not only for the fun of whirling around but for the social interaction.

In those days I had refused to use my diabetes as an excuse for not doing things. Now, I didn't want to use my blindness as an excuse. I was determined to do whatever I wanted to do, and I wanted to dance.

These monthly dances were a flurry of activity. On stage a live band would reel out foot-stomping fiddle and guitar music while a caller called out dance instructions. On the dance floor there were usually about a hundred people divided into eight-person squares. The dances involved a fairly complex set of maneuvers. An inexperienced dancer could throw a whole square into total confusion.

I was familiar with a lot of the dances, and I felt I could do well if I could hear the caller. I knew how to position myself for the dances based on the direction from the caller and the voices of the people around me. My main problem would be that I couldn't help correct for anyone else's errors.

At my first dance as a blind person, the caller decided to call a "hey for four," a complex dance that involved weaving in and out of other dancers in a figure eight. It was unclear how a blind person could even participate.

My good friends, recognizing that this was going to be a difficult dance for me, formed a square of expert dancers so no one would mess up the square, and so they could help me get through it. As the music started, I found myself in the iron grip of my dance partner, Laura May, a woman who was determined that I would be successful. She bodily twisted me, turning me one way and then the other to get me through the weave. It was truly like surrendering my life to a higher power. There was no doubt in my mind that we were doing fine. When it was over I was a bit dizzy, momentarily confused about the male/female role reversal, and starting to enjoy myself.

Most of the people I danced with over the course of the evening had no idea I couldn't see because I didn't carry my white cane, and I was wearing regular glasses. As the dances progressed, I would usually get to where I was supposed to be, but I couldn't reach out and hook up with my successive partners. People would come along, see me staring into space, and then just grab me and swing me around. It was funny but also rather intimidating. I was in the center of a good deal of confusion over the course of the night. The redeeming factor was that everyone was there to have fun. I would remind myself of that over and over.

My friends thought it was great that I was willing to try dancing blind. They also enjoyed the comedy of my efforts, the way my squares would gradually fall apart, and the challenge of trying to keep the squares together.

A Victory of Sorts

The positive feelings I got from dancing made me want to try other things. I asked Kenny what he thought about going skiing, and he said it sounded like a great idea. It was wintertime in Alaska, and almost everyone I knew was skiing.

I decided to go cross-country skiing at Hatcher Pass, a mountainous, backcountry ski area that was a two-hour drive from Anchorage. I had skied the pass a number of times before I went blind, so I was familiar with the terrain.

Kenny (on the right) and I at the Formal Spring Ski Party at Hatcher Pass, Alaska

I also had a good friend, Steve, a recreational therapist, who was willing to ski with me. Kenny and some other friends would provide additional support.

As we drove up to Hatcher Pass, Kenny commented on a blizzard that he said was closing in on the pass. A blizzard wouldn't stop us from skiing, but it would reduce visibility for my sighted guides and add a level of risk.

As I stepped from the car into the stinging wind and snow, I felt my stomach knot up. Trying to let go of my fear, I clipped into my skis and followed Steve's voice off into the cold.

Coaching me verbally, he tried to keep me on the few trails there were. "Now turn right, now turn left, keep a little more to the left . . ."

I had trouble staying in Steve's tracks, and I fell so often that each struggle to get back up out of the deep powder became a major exertion. As we traveled, I felt increasingly intimidated by the varying terrain and disturbed that I was burdening my group. I felt uncomfortable to be getting so much help. I was not used to so much attention, and it made me uneasy. As I struggled up after each fall, I began to notice that I was shaking, but I didn't know whether it was from cold, physical exhaustion, or fear.

Two hours after setting out, I sat high up on the boulder-strewn ridge, sweaty and exhausted. As I sat there, I began to realize that what we had just done was the easy part. The way back was downhill through the boulder field. Fear welled up inside me again.

To distract myself, I made a goal that on the run back to the small A-frame lodge where we had started, I would fall less than twenty times. As I started back, I picked up speed too quickly and found myself picturing boulders in my path, so I would deliberately fall to slow myself down. Despite Steve's coaching, I kept falling and bruising myself, and I got more and more tired.

The afternoon seemed to wear on forever. Occasionally I would call out into the wind-driven snow, and if no one answered, I'd feel a shock of panic that I was lost.

When I finally heard Steve announce that we were back at the lodge, I felt enormous relief. And, I'd fallen only seventeen times! It was a victory of sorts. As I hobbled into the lodge, snow-covered, white cane in hand, people came up to congratulate me and applaud my willingness to ski blind. It didn't sink in. All I could think was, "I can't believe I was crazy enough to try something like that."

Reflecting that my first ski trip as a blind person may have been a victory, but not a fun one, I signed up for skiing classes with Alpine Alternatives, a handicap recreation organization in Anchorage. There, I learned to find the tracks with my skis, to shift my weight so that every bump didn't dump me, and to carve downhill "telemark" turns. Skiing blind remained a challenge, but my fear was mostly gone. I skied several more times that winter, both cross-country and downhill.

Growing Confidence

That same night, one of the cooks who was working in the lodge cut his thumb. He was in the bathroom cleaning up his cut when Kenny saw the bleeding and suggested that he have me examine it. When Kenny came and got me, I felt excited to be asked to help and confident of my ability to do so.

I told the cook I was a doctor, that I was blind, and that I would feel his wound to determine its severity. I knew it was important to determine whether or not he needed stitches. By the sound of his voice, I could tell he was doing okay. I washed my hands and checked the wound. Probing the tip of his thumb, I asked if he could feel my hand. He said yes, and I knew he had not severed a major nerve. I asked if the tip of the thumb had a good pink color. It did, he said, and I knew he had not severed an artery. After lightly feeling the wound to determine its size, I turned to my brother and asked, "How deep is it, Kenny?"

"It's the deepest cut I've ever seen," he answered in an overly loud voice, clearly overly upset.

At this point the cook started feeling woozy and had to sit down. It was still snowing and dark outside, and it was a slick, difficult drive down the steep, winding mountain road to a hospital. Still, I recommended that the cook go to the hospital for stitches.

When the cook returned later that evening, he thanked me and bought me a beer. It was the first time I'd actually practiced medicine since I'd gone blind, and the beer was my first income. It felt wonderful to help in that way again. This was yet another demonstration that it wasn't my eyesight but my knowledge of medicine that made me a capable doctor. I felt a growing confidence in my ability to practice medicine again.

Back home, I worked on my resume and made job inquiries. My blind colleagues from the American Society of Handicapped Physicians would call from time to time to talk and offer reassurance. I became convinced that I would be going back to work soon.

Choosing Happiness

In December 1984, I flew to Los Angeles to spend Christmas with my brother Stephen and other family members who came for the holiday. For my first blind Christmas my mother loaded me up with "blind presents"—a compact tape recorder, a braille labeling machine, a talking watch, and a talking calculator.

Family gatherings at Christmas were common. In this photo taken in Kentucky, I helped Stephen show off two of his presents. He had started a recording company called Mountain Railroad Records, so gifts for him often featured trains.

Energized by the warm California sun and the support of my family, I began to think about running again. I hadn't run in the seven months since my eye doctor had advised me to stop. His advice to stop running had been reasonable enough from his perspective, but for me it amounted to living in fear of life. Physical activity gave me joy, a desire to live. Without regular exercise, I had gained ten pounds, and I'd had trouble keeping my blood sugar levels normal.

Perhaps I had let my doctor make a decision that was really mine to make. I wanted to feel happy again. I wanted to take greater control of my life and my diabetes. I decided to start running again, even if it increased the chance of further hemorrhaging in my eyes.

On a warm summery day in January, Stephen and I walked down to the bike path at Venice Beach. I walked about a half step behind him, holding his elbow. When we reached the bike path he started into a jog, and I fell into step with him. We ran for the better part of an hour, slowly, dodging bicyclists and walkers, enjoying the ocean breezes.

Stephen even saw actress Cameron Diaz run past us going the other way. That was a star sighting that I missed seeing. But even so, it was an hour of real joy for me, a step back toward happiness. It seemed very important to Stephen also, to help me in this way. A few days later we ran again.

Then, one morning in mid-January, still on vacation in California, I woke up to find that I could tell the window from the closet. One was brighter than the other. The hemorrhage in my right eye was beginning to clear.

9

Light

> *Human misery must somewhere have a stop: There is no wind that always blows a storm.*
> —Euripides, *Alcestis*

My new ability to "see" the light from my bed in Stephen's Los Angeles apartment did not seem initially remarkable. In the four months since I had gone totally blind, I had been able to sense the presence of light on occasion. Usually, it was in the morning when I woke up. I would attribute the improvement to my visualization exercises. "My vision is getting better," I would reassure myself. But each time, as I got out of bed and began to move around, the red blood cells that might have settled overnight would get stirred back up, and everything would turn black again.

One morning after several weeks, I lay in bed and enjoyed my ability to see the window. I couldn't really "see" the window, of course. All I could do was see that there was brightness in the direction of the window compared to looking the opposite way toward a blank black wall. I got up and began to move around, and nothing changed. I was able to recognize sources of light all that day, and the next, and the next. I was guardedly optimistic. I didn't know exactly what it meant, and I didn't want to be too disappointed if my vision went totally black again.

The improvement in my light perception over the next few days was so gradual as to be almost unnoticeable. Then one morning I found that I could recognize not only light but hazy forms. It was hard to suppress my excitement. I had never heard of anything like this happening in cases of diabetic blindness. I reminded myself that the bleeding could restart at any time and leave me blind again.

I felt that my decision to start running again had contributed very directly to the physical healing that was taking place. It was true that I was acting contrary to the medical advice I had received. But I felt like the combined emotional and physical benefits of running far outweighed the risk of jarring my retinal blood vessels and causing bleeding. My decision to run had brought me back in touch with the health, happiness, excitement, and control I'd felt in my running days. I had no doubt that restimulating these positive emotions would help my body heal if anything would.

Leaving the California sunshine and returning to the Alaskan midwinter, I found a major flaw in my plan to run every day. It was hard to motivate myself or anyone else to go out into the cold winter darkness for a run. Seeking a solution to this problem one evening, Kenny and I, still roommates, settled on a plan. We agreed to exercise a minimum of three times a week for the next twelve weeks. Whichever one of us failed to do so owed the other person one hundred dollars. Given our modest lifestyles, the money would provide tremendous motivation.

I bought warm running gear and steel-pronged ice grippers for my running shoes, and we began running on the snowy backstreets near our house. I would run slowly at Kenny's elbow. After a couple of weeks, I could see shapes well enough that I didn't need to hold his elbow. But I still needed him to coach me verbally or take my arm if I was coming to something I couldn't see, like a curb or lamppost.

For many weeks my body felt sluggish and slow, and the runs were hard. There wasn't much that felt good about my running program, just the slight moral gratification of sticking to my commitment and the fact that I hadn't lost my hundred dollars yet. As I compared my overweight and underused body to its leaner, faster, former self, I had to remind myself that I wasn't training for a race, and I didn't have to run far or fast. I was just running for myself, for my diabetic control, for my happiness.

When I told my eye doctor that I had started running again, he was supportive of my decision in spite of his earlier recommendation. He pointed out that there was no conclusive evidence that vigorous exercise caused retinal bleeding. I joked that my exercise couldn't really be called "vigorous" just yet.

About this time, I met with the directors of the school for the blind and asked for time off. I'd been enrolled in the school for about five months, but for two weeks my vision in my right eye had gradually been improving, and I really felt as though I didn't need to continue to learn the skills for the blind. I was certain I wasn't going to need them. I didn't want to burn any bridges, but I fully intended to drop out of blind school unless the need for it came up again later.

Since I was still almost totally blind, and the retinal bleeding could start again at any time, they were surprised by my request. But I was more convinced than ever that my sight was coming back. I told them I wanted to spend less time studying for blindness and more time trying to find a job.

They were reluctant to give me the time off. They felt my skills for dealing with blindness were still inadequate, and that if I didn't work on them, I would eventually have problems. In their experience, students who left their school with inadequate skills never mastered those skills and found themselves at a great disadvantage in life.

I answered this with the argument that I had significantly more training than any of the other students. As a doctor, I didn't need to know how to read braille because I could earn enough money to hire a reader. I was hardheaded in my optimism. I wanted to get on with my life. I wanted to work, not live off social security. The school directors probably considered my optimism unfounded at this point, but they could see that I knew what I wanted. They finally granted the time off.

Quieting Doubt

One February morning as I was working around the house I shared with Kenny, suddenly my good eye began to bleed, and within moments I was totally blind again. I was stunned. I had been so sure that my sight was coming back. I sat in my front room in the darkness, hurting and overwhelmed with self-doubt. Maybe I'd just been clinging to a fantasy. Maybe permanent blindness was inevitable, and everyone but me had known that for a long time. Maybe the school directors had been right about wanting to keep me in classes. Maybe my doctor had been right all along about not running. Maybe the clearing of my vision had not been a sign of healing but just another step on the way to permanent blindness. Maybe I was totally out of touch with reality.

My spiral of negative thoughts plunged me into deep despair. Finally, I found my white cane and tapped my way back to the living room couch. I sat dazed and completely defeated. I was still sitting in the living room when Kenny came home from work that evening. He noticed the white cane and asked what was wrong.

"I've gone blind again," I told him and began crying. He came over and put his arms around me. As we sat there, I could feel sobs shaking Kenny's body, almost as though he had been the one who had gone blind.

The cold dark days of February seemed to go on forever. They mirrored the harshness and despair I felt inside. As I sank deeper and deeper into depression, I eventually began to realize that my doubts and fears were feeding on themselves; they'd never stop unless I stopped them. They were exhausting me and creating an emotional environment that could only lead to greater pain and illness.

I began to meet these doubts and fears by refusing to entertain them. Whenever I noticed such thoughts using up my mental energy, I would simply recognize what was happening, let the thoughts go, and return my mind to matters at hand. I was not trying to create a world totally free of doubt. I just wanted to be in control of doubt rather than having it control me. I wanted to deal consciously with real issues, not fears.

In spite of my best efforts to focus on other things, troublesome mental fantasies came frequently, but I did not berate myself for having these thoughts. They showed up on their own, and I tried just to gently let them go. Self-criticism would have defeated my efforts to create a positive frame of mind.

When my fearful emotions seemed to be gaining the upper hand, I would find a quiet place and meditate. My meditation often took the form of concentration on my breath. As I sat with eyes closed, all sorts of thoughts would arise, particularly my anxieties about blindness. Each time an uninvited thought arose, I would gently bring my mind back to my breathing.

This kind of meditation not only eased the mental burden I had been carrying, but it also seemed to put me in touch with a deeper part of myself. This deeper part seemed wiser, more loving, calmer, and more reassuring than my day-to-day self. In the calmness induced by this kind of meditation, I could view my relapse more realistically, and this enabled me to decide affirmatively, "I can heal my blindness again. I've just had a setback."

These sessions were very reassuring, but even the reassurance itself was fuel for my doubts. "What if one of these days I can't convince myself that I'm going to be okay?" my automatic pilot would say, and I would feel that familiar dread and division inside. Then it would be time, once again, for me to recognize doubt and let it go or find a quiet place and meditate.

I would bolster my belief that I could heal my blindness by reminding myself of the studies that indicated how important a role personal belief can play in healing. I focused on my successes and on the steps I was taking to heal. I continued meditating, doing visualizations, and running every day. These things made me feel like I was taking care of myself, healing myself. My eye improved.

By March I could again see some light. I viewed the improvements cautiously. Within a couple of weeks, I could make out forms and shapes again, and move around without my cane.

Practicing Medicine

After I could see well enough to walk, I started attending staff meetings at the hospital where I had been granted privileges. I used the meetings as an opportunity to talk to various doctors informally and see if they or anyone they knew needed help.

When I was trying to figure out how I was going to work as a doctor again, I had a couple of pivotal moments. The first was when I heard that Alaska Pacific University (APU) was starting up a master's program for nurse practitioners, and they needed faculty. I knew I was perfectly suited for that job because I did not need vision to transfer all of my medical knowledge to those students.

Another major "aha" moment was when I thought about the Alaska Native Hospital, which was run by the Indian Health Service. In the remote villages where there were no doctors, the health aides in those communities consulted with a doctor at the Anchorage hospital by radio or phone to relay information and get advice. The doctor on call advised the health aides how to stabilize the patients and what to do to take care of them. The health aides only had about three months of training. They could take vital signs and assess situations that required first aid, but they had to speak to a doctor at the hospital to get better insight. I realized that I could be that doctor on the radio.

The positive actions I took to network and think about possibilities I hadn't considered before helped me understand that there were multiple ways in which I could continue my career as a medical doctor. Buoyed with both conviction and confidence, I knew the right job would be there for me.

In March 1985, I heard that MedAlaska, a new clinic in town, needed doctors. The clinic had an emergency room and a family practice under the same roof. I sent in my resume. A few days later I got a call to come in for an interview.

During interviews with three of the clinic doctors, I was asked many questions about my qualifications. When I told them I was recovering from blindness, and that I was still visually impaired, they expressed concern about my ability to examine patients. I assured them that I could see well enough to do most routine physical exams. They asked how I would handle exams that required sharp vision, for example retinal exams. I suggested we have a physician's assistant do any exams that required visual acuity.

I was sure I could do the job, and that I could compensate adequately for things I couldn't do. I was grateful for their willingness to discuss their concerns openly. I was delighted when they finally said they were willing to try me out.

In March, I went to work and found the people at the clinic to be tremendously supportive. Initially, I had difficulty finding a nurse on the staff who had the kind of experience I needed to compensate for my visual impairment. Being new myself, I was hesitant to risk offending anyone by suggesting that I hire a new nurse. About the fifth week of work, after I'd returned from a short vacation, I found that one of the physician's assistants had gone to bat for me in my absence and obtained permission for me to interview and hire my own nurse. I felt very grateful.

Later that week I hired Andy. Andy not only had good nursing experience, but she was also adventurous, outdoorsy, and energetic. I liked her immediately. I soon found that Andy's energy, skill, and compassion made my work easy. Everything I needed to continue in medical practice now seemed to be in place. I felt that my decision to value myself by taking my time to find the right work opportunity had paid off.

I thought back to the day I went blind and my fears about being destitute. I remembered how many times such fears had drained my energy. I realized again that such fears are only thoughts, not reality. Reality is a combination of the little things we do day to day, and it is the best indicator of where we are going.

As I had worked on my resume and looked for the right job and moved ahead with my life, I had been creating my reality. Being able to continue in family practice was very reaffirming. It added to my sense that everything would be okay. I resolved in the future not to get so caught up in the drama and dark fantasy world that fear can create.

I continued to run, and running continued to be difficult. Sometime in April, Kenny and I signed off on our running bet. We had both won. I was delighted that our bet had successfully launched my effort to get back into good shape. I was now running four or five times a week, and I felt that from here on, there was no stopping me.

As the weather got warmer and piles of snow turned into slush, I would splash along through puddles enjoying the balmy warmth of spring and the growing strength in my body. Now I was running for love, not money, and it seemed to get easier. I started running along a bike trail that skirted the ocean, the Coastal Trail, and I enjoyed the fact that I could now distinguish the water from the city skyline.

Navigation and Inspiration

Just a few days before the annual meeting of the American Society of Handicapped Physicians in Anaheim, California, which I had planned to attend, I went blind again. Emotionally, this was difficult, as always. The timing of this setback, however, was something of a blessing in disguise. I went ahead and flew down to the conference blind, making my way around with my white cane.

At the conference I got tremendous support from other members of the society, a number of whom were permanently blind. I still didn't believe my blindness would be permanent. This belief gave me a sense of optimism and a sense of greater possibilities.

I was introduced to a doctor whom I'll call Alex. Alex had been severely crippled in a climbing accident. Brain damage from the accident had left him unable to speak although he could hear and think very clearly. He got around in a motorized wheelchair, and on his lap he carried a magnetic board with all the letters of the alphabet affixed. He would respond to conversation by spelling out words or just pointing to letters in sequence. It was a painfully slow process. I heard from others about his accident and how his fiancée had been killed at the same time.

After the accident, Alex had undergone an extended period of rehabilitation. Then, working out the necessary adjustments to his medical routine, he had gone back to practicing medicine. He gave me a detailed medical history form he had his clients fill out, a form he used to assess and diagnose problems. It was a careful and thorough form, one that would be a credit to any doctor. I felt overwhelmed at how much he had overcome, how small my problems were by comparison, and how indomitable his spirit was.

To walk, Alex needed the support of a strong person. He would move ahead by leaning his weight on a support person, lurching one leg forward, and then launching his body out at about a 45-degree angle to his first step. Each step was in a different direction.

During one session break, he and I and another physician who was wheelchair-bound decided to go to lunch together. Wanting to walk, Alex leaned on me for support and proceeded to launch himself forward. Still blind, I held onto the other physician's wheelchair for direction, and with our wheelchair man navigating, we headed off.

As we rolled, groped, and lurched toward the restaurant I had to smile at the spectacle we must have presented. I was enjoying our physical connection as we traveled, and I felt grateful that we had an organization that gave me the opportunity to support others and be supported.

The guest speaker at our conference was Dr. Albert Sabin, the man who developed the oral polio vaccine, which has been one of the major contributions to health on our planet. Dr. Sabin gave us statistics about how many children were still dying of polio and described his recent travels by bush plane into the jungles of Brazil where he was helping to administer the vaccine to native populations that had not been treated.

What struck me was that although Dr. Sabin was eighty years old, he was still out on the front lines doing menial and physical work that he could have left to others. I made a decision at that meeting that I wanted to have that same kind of vitality and conviction about my own life's work.

Healing From Within, Help From Without

I went blind five times during 1985. Once, I was simply leaning over to tie my shoe when I coughed, and the pressure of the cough on my eyes caused everything to go black again.

Initially, each hemorrhage was emotionally devastating. Each time I would go through the crying and the upset, and I'd wonder if I might really stay blind. During these times, I was fortunate to have the support of friends, particularly my brother Kenny and my nurse, Andy. In their presence I could cry and talk about my feelings and experience the same kind of emotional healing an injured child feels crawling into the comforting arms of a sympathetic parent.

After talking and crying, I would be in a place where I could let go of my fears and realize, "Okay, I've handled this before, and I intend to handle it this time." Resolving to clear the bleeding again, I would continue to do everything I could do to heal—running, visualizing, and keeping my blood sugar levels normal.

Reflecting on emotional outbreaks and the calm that followed, I realized that as adults, we often deny ourselves the opportunity for emotional healing that makes childhood such a rich experience. As young children we let our bodies shake with tears, laughter, fear, and anger, and thereby we experience a healthy emotional release. As we get older, we find that none of these natural expressions, except laughter, are socially acceptable. We learn to deny or shut down our emotions, to numb ourselves against them.

If a boy cries, he is told not to be a "baby." Anger is considered bad, and fear is weak. All of a sudden, emotions that are honest and natural and healthy are not okay. So we learn to pretend that we don't feel, and we let hurts that can no longer be healed by natural expression damage our health through detachment or suppressed anger.

The social practice of shutting down and denying feelings is based on our fear of being burdened by other people's emotions and the belief that a person's sadness or anger will go away if it's not expressed. However, if someone else is sad, it does not mean that we have to be sad, nor does it mean that we have to be uncomfortable until we have fixed the problem so that everyone is happy again. Furthermore, emotions that are suppressed do not just vanish. I was lucky to have friends that, in some sense, understood my need for support rather than judgment when I was feeling fear or anger or despair.

A Blind Physician

One of the frightening things to me about my episodes of blindness was that I was working and treating patients at this time. After my first recurrence of blindness, I didn't know whether to try to take time off and upset the office schedule or risk returning to work and deal with questions as to whether I was fit to practice. How could I reassure the patients and the other doctors when I was in such despair myself?

I confided my problem to my nurse, Andy. She made it clear that she would help me in any way she could. We worked out a system where she would go in and talk to the patients first, get their weight, take their blood pressure and pulse, and do whatever else was needed to prepare them for my exam. Then she would ask them to sit on the examining room table. This was so I would know where to direct my attention when I entered the room. In parting, she would mention that I was having some trouble with my vision.

I would then come in and announce that I was having trouble with my vision today but that it would not affect my ability to take care of whatever their concern was—their pain, stomachache, cold, sore throat, or whatever. If there were visual aspects to the exam, Andy would come back in and assist me.

The patients were very accepting of this, and some even had questions about what my vision problem was. I would tell them it was bad vision from diabetes, and that I expected it to clear up. I was able to get most of my diagnostic information by taking a careful history, listening to the heart and lungs, feeling the belly, or whatever was called for. I think many of my patients didn't realize that I was totally blind at the time.

I never shared my predicament with the other doctors at the clinic. I was still very afraid that they might think I couldn't do the job. My rationale for not bringing it up was that the patients were responding well to me, my nurse was very supportive, and people were getting better. I felt I was working quite well and didn't want prejudice to derail me. My vision loss from these hemorrhages would usually last about two weeks before clearing to a point where I could consider myself just visually impaired, not totally blind.

It was a difficult year. The only positive aspect I could see at the time was that I was making it through the blind periods until I experienced clearing, all the while feeling like I could heal myself. I was also getting better at dealing with my despair. After each hemorrhage, I was able to emotionally bounce back more easily.

A Kindred Spirit

In early October 1985, I had another hemorrhage, the fifth one that year. I knew the repeated hemorrhages were occurring because the capillary blood vessels were so fragile it was easy for one to break and cause another bleeding episode. I did see my eye doctor occasionally, and he said this was just the normal course of events. Although frustrated at the setback, I felt that I now had good evidence that I could and would recover.

One day, two friends called to invite me to attend the awards banquet sponsored by the Governor's Committee on Employment of the Handicapped.

My friends, Nanette and Lulie, both worked for agencies serving the disabled, and they knew I was interested in their work. Being blind again, I felt disappointed that I'd be listening to descriptions of the banquet hall and the people in attendance rather than seeing them for myself.

The banquet was held in the ballroom of one of the large downtown hotels in Anchorage, and it was a gala event. Awards were given for the handicapped employer of the year among other distinctions. The climax of the evening was the presentation of the award for the Handicapped Alaskan of the Year. The emcee introduced the Alaskan of the Year as a healer by profession and a person who had contributed a lot to his community. In addition, we learned he was a backpacker, a skier, and a tireless dancer.

"Ah, a kindred spirit," I thought. I liked him already.

Then the emcee added that the Handicapped Alaskan of the Year had run the Boston Marathon nine times.

The emcee was losing credibility with me here. I began to disbelieve that anyone in this room could have run the Boston Marathon nine times as I had.

When the emcee then asked me to come forward, I was stunned, and I understood for the first time that he had been talking about me! I had never realized that what I was doing mattered to anyone but myself and my close friends. Now I was about to receive an award that said that what I was doing was important to my community, that I was making a contribution. I was overwhelmed.

I felt so excited that I made my way to the stage with almost no help. It seemed like I was walking above the ballroom floor, and I was tempted to jump up on the stage when I knew I was approaching it, but I resisted. Arriving at the microphone, I was handed a bronze plaque. All I could think of was my tremendous appreciation for those who had helped me along the way.

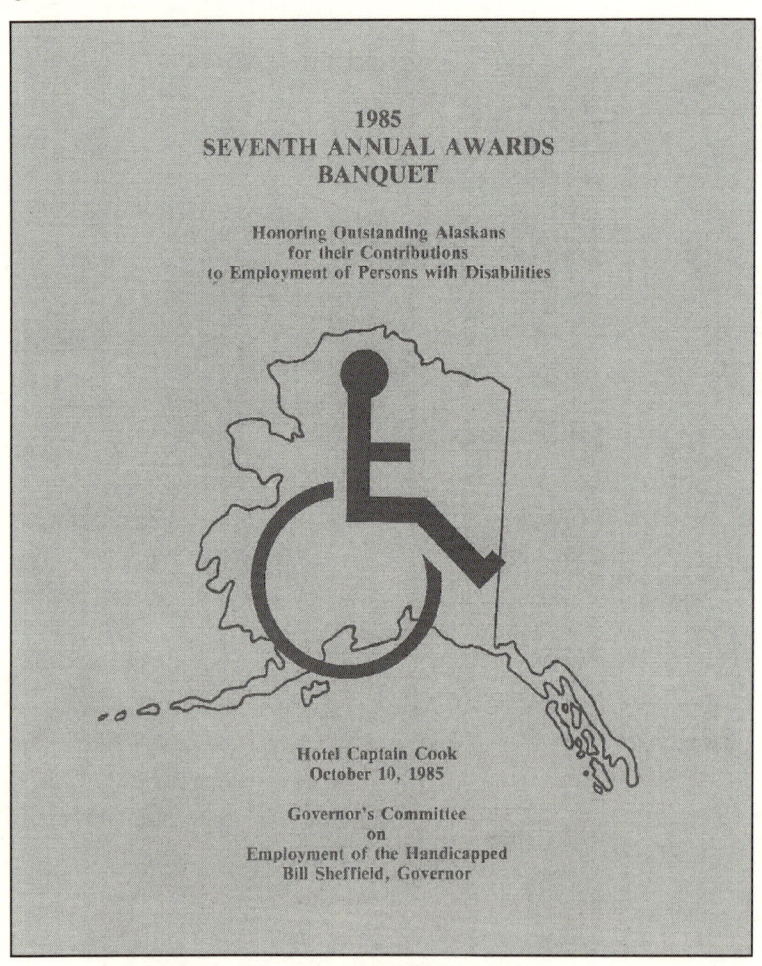

Program cover from the 1985 awards banquet

Looking Good, Sounding Bad

One year after I had received the 1985 award for Handicapped Alaskan of the Year, I was invited to present the nominees for the award for 1986. I was becoming accustomed to speaking to small groups of people with diabetes, so I wasn't overly intimidated by the prospect of speaking to a crowd.

The awards banquet was orchestrated somewhat like the Academy Awards for the film industry. My job was to tell a little bit about myself and then to introduce each of the nominees with a brief description of their situation, and what they were doing to overcome their handicap.

I told the emcee that it was important for me to get the name and description for each nominee well in advance of the banquet so that I could familiarize myself with the material. I didn't divulge that I planned to memorize it so that I wouldn't have to struggle with trying to read it aloud. My reading was very halting and broken because of my limited vision.

Unfortunately, I didn't get the written materials until the day before the banquet. To make it worse, there were thirteen nominees, which meant there were thirteen paragraphs and names to memorize. I just couldn't memorize it all in one day and resolved instead to read it out loud at the banquet. I thought I could pull it off.

The large banquet hall of the Hotel Captain Cook felt very much like the Great Hall of the castles I had visited in Scotland. It was a wonderful setting for a banquet and awards ceremony, but it intimidated me. I comforted myself with the reassurance that at least I had the ability to tell my own story without referring to notes. And in my rented tuxedo, I felt confident that I could look good.

When it was finally my turn to speak, I rattled off a brief version of my blindness story without a hitch. Then it came time to announce the nominees, and I had to start reading. It was terribly hard for me to try to read that material. I hesitated often and mispronounced words. I apologized and tried to keep going. When I realized I had read the word "therapist" as "the rapist," I wanted to give up and hand the papers over to anyone else who could read them.

After a seemingly endless period of embarrassment and feelings of shame, I finally finished. I slunk back to my table feeling like a terrible failure and an even worse performer. I wished that I could just disappear, or that I could just wake up and discover it was all a bad dream.

My friend, Steve, who had taken me skiing blind, was sitting next to me at my table. I told him how disappointed I was in my presentation. He could probably tell how I felt from the way my head drooped and shoulders hung.

His response shocked me. He told me it was a very meaningful and inspiring presentation and a testimony to my courage. I thought he was just trying to make me feel better until he explained.

He pointed out that when I was standing up there speaking easily about my experiences with blindness without much emotion and wearing that elegant tuxedo, it was like empty words. It didn't seem real or genuine. When I had to struggle and stumble and falter with my reading and feelings of embarrassment, I became real. My story became believable and genuine, and the struggle I had experienced became palpable in the room.

He said that he was moved by my demonstration and could see that it had been moving to many others in the banquet hall. All eyes had been fixed on me, and some were wet with tears. For the few moments I was up there, those in the room could experience the hardship of living with a handicap and the perseverance of prevailing.

Despite his encouragement and wisdom, I was still shaken. I didn't like sounding that bad or feeling that ashamed, even if it did give my message more impact.

10

Run River Run

*If you've been thinking you're all that you've got,
Then don't feel alone anymore.
When we're together then you've got a lot,
'Cause I am the river and you are the shore.*
—Loggins & Messina, "Watching the River Run"

The vision in my one good eye started to clear after the October 1985 hemorrhage. I was again able to recognize light and dark. That was enough for me to be able to find my way around in unfamiliar surroundings without a cane. Eventually I developed one small space in my field of vision where I could read letters on the 20/60 line of the eye chart. My vision was still so spotty and splotchy that I couldn't recognize a bicycle if one were set in front of me, but I could read the brand name on the cross bar—one letter at a time. I had a window of light into the world. I could see.

While my vision was improving, my work situation was deteriorating. The clinic where I worked was having serious financial difficulty, so the staff was asked to accept large pay cuts.

I could tell that the clinic was going to go under, and I wondered what I should do. If I went to work somewhere else, I was almost certain to face again the prejudice about my vision. I could understand having to demonstrate my competence, but the thought of being denied work and professional advancement for no logical reason left me feeling irritated and tired.

I considered opening my own private practice. I had been in private practice in Kentucky for several years just after finishing my residency, so the idea of opening a practice was not by itself intimidating. The harder question was whether I should start my own practice given my visual impairment. I had been treating patients while I was blind, so in the final analysis the idea of starting a practice with some vision seemed reasonable and possible.

I asked my nurse, Andy, if she would come with me. She had no hesitation. She was concerned about her own job security at the clinic, and we had an excellent working relationship. We decided to launch out on our own. We opened an office in Anchorage with another family doctor who was also leaving the clinic and began building a clientele.

Shortly after we opened our office, I did a 24-hour urine collection test on myself to check if my kidneys were functioning normally. I had been giving myself this test every four months since medical school as a precaution. Diabetic kidney disease is one of the complications that can result from having type 1 diabetes that begins in adolescence. I wanted to know immediately if my kidneys started showing any signs of failure so that I could do whatever might be possible to prevent further deterioration.

This time I was very disturbed to find that the test results were abnormal. I repeated the test, and the results were again abnormal. My "creatinine clearance," which is the ability of the kidneys to clear the waste product creatinine from the blood, had dropped by half, and the amount of creatinine in my blood had gone up about 70 percent. I was very concerned. All that I had learned about diabetic kidney disease flooded my mind.

I had been taught in medical school that when creatinine clearance diminishes to the degree that mine had, the kidneys were already severely damaged and would last only about eighteen months. Since the body can't clear waste products from the blood once the kidneys fail, normal physical activity becomes difficult, and participation in sports or other rigorous exercise becomes practically impossible. Lack of exercise causes further deterioration in health. A very restricted diet was required to eliminate protein-rich foods, which are hard for the body to process.

Kidney dialysis was also required. This meant that a person must be hooked to a machine three times a week for four to five hours per session so that the blood could be removed from the body and mechanically cleaned before it was transfused back into the bloodstream. I knew that dialysis was very stressful on the body and often caused acute nausea. Some people had died of a heart attack due to the stress of dialysis.

But I knew dialysis wasn't even an option for me. At that time, dialysis in type 1 diabetes carried a 50 percent mortality rate in the first year, and because of the poor outcomes, dialysis wasn't even offered to people with type 1 diabetes.

The alternative to dialysis was a kidney transplant. The wait to find a donor could last as much as a year or two. After the transplant, the patient would need to take immunosuppressant drugs for the rest of his or her life to keep the body from rejecting the new kidney. Those drugs often caused severe nausea and vomiting as a side effect.

One of the drugs, cortisone, could cause edema or swelling of body tissues. Cortisone also counteracted insulin, which made control of blood sugar levels very difficult for someone with diabetes. Even then, there was no guarantee that the body would accept the new kidney.

But again, I knew this treatment approach wasn't really an option for me. As a diabetic, I would traditionally have been rejected as a candidate for a transplant. This is because diabetics' bodies have difficulty fighting infection and because the immunosuppressants necessary for a transplant created an even greater risk of infection.

I felt like I had just been handed a death sentence. If my kidneys failed, I wasn't sure I wanted to live. I thought of myself as an athlete and a professional person. I savored feeling healthy and productive. If my kidneys failed, I felt that my health would be too poor to continue to practice medicine. Without healthy kidneys, I couldn't do all the active things I loved to do, and I would have to be taken care of.

I didn't think I could face that. I had beaten blindness and prejudice against the blind. I couldn't believe that I had overcome so much only to lose it all to kidney failure. I didn't think I had the emotional strength to face all these new losses. I considered borrowing money so that I could travel around the world and experience it fully before I lost my ability to do so.

I went to see a kidney specialist. He confirmed that what I had learned in medical school about total kidney failure occurring in eighteen months was the traditional understanding. However, he said that recent studies had shown that a protein-restricted diet could slow and perhaps halt kidney deterioration. I was relieved to hear that there was hope. He cautioned me that going on a protein-restricted diet meant cutting back substantially on the amount of protein-rich foods that most people were accustomed to eating. "I'm not saying that you can never eat meat again," he clarified. "You just have to watch the amounts."

I'd have given up meat in an instant to save my kidneys. I went immediately to see a dietician and was put on a 40-gram protein diet. It was not the most severe diet that can be prescribed for kidney failure, but it was a definite change from how I had been eating. I was restricted to eating only two protein-rich foods a day. For example, I could have two eggs, or two glasses of milk, or two slices of cheese, or two slices of bologna. The rest of my diet consisted primarily of fruits, vegetables, and grains. I followed the diet religiously and hoped for the best.

Willing to Be Happier

Two weeks after starting my new diet I attended my first personal growth seminar. I had been hearing about these types of seminars for some time from friends who had attended them. My initial response when I was approached about taking the seminar was that it cost a lot of money and that I didn't really need anything like that. I considered myself to be a well-adjusted and happy person.

One friend finally convinced me when she asked, "Even if you don't think you need it, are you willing to be happier?"

I decided to attend the seminar partly out of curiosity, partly to placate friends, and partly on the outside chance that I might get something useful out of it.

The seminar focused on exploring feelings about self-worth and relationships with others. It had a very profound impact on me. It created an awareness of the powerful influence of the emotions and belief systems that I had assumed as a child. I realized that I continued to be governed by these influences, even though many of them did not serve me well. For example, I still felt at some level that if I did things purely for my own happiness and enjoyment that that was wrong.

I began to see how many times in the past I had sabotaged my own happiness because of unexamined and unhealthy personal beliefs. It is ironic for me to look back now and see

My brother Kenny and my new friend Ellen clogging during a dance performance at a musical festival in Alaska

how depressed and fearful I was at this time, and yet before the seminar I had considered myself to be too emotionally healthy to have any real need for it. My self-awareness increased so much after the first seminar that I began taking others.

Four months after my initial abnormal kidney test result, I was feeling very happy and energetic and didn't know exactly what to attribute it to. I thought it might be because of the new awareness that I had acquired in the personal growth seminars. But I had also met a woman at the monthly dances whom I was very infatuated with, Ellen, who was part of Kenny's clogging group. I wondered if that would be a better explanation for my new-found energy.

The other possibility was that my new protein-restricted diet was working. When I ran, I felt unusually strong. Before I had started the diet, I would go out for a three- or four-mile run and come back feeling tired. Now I felt I could go farther. I also felt lighter and faster.

I had the creatinine clearance test done again. Not only had the deterioration of my kidneys stopped, but my kidney function had returned to normal. I was elated! I had done what was necessary to heal myself once again. Anxiety and doubt were replaced by confidence and energy. I felt back in control of my life. The death sentence had been lifted.

Chariots of Fire

I felt so good that I began toying with a new idea. I had stopped running marathons six years before because I no longer had the energy to run that far. I was later told by the kidney specialist that my loss of energy was due to the kidney disease. I had started running again after I went blind, but I had never gone back to long-distance runs. I didn't feel that I had the stamina or strength to do them. I felt that I couldn't demand too much of myself physically; I had to be realistic about my health and limit my expectations. Now I had some sight and revitalized kidneys. Why not run a marathon again?

I made an agreement with my new friend Ellen to run with her in a marathon coming up in June 1987, eight months away. This would leave plenty of time for training. I had been running three to five miles four or five times a week. Gradually I worked up to running between five and ten miles a day every day. Breaking ten miles was a real milestone. It had been six years since I had run that far. After I had worked up to ten miles, Ellen and I started doing a long slow run once a week. We started at twelve miles and worked up to eighteen. Every run brought back old memories. My endurance and stamina seemed to be coming back just like it had been before.

The racecourse lay along a beautifully wooded trail. The day of the race was cool and overcast. My brother Kenny positioned himself to hand me my drink bottles at the five-, ten-, fifteen-, and twenty-mile marks. During the first five miles of the race, I felt tired and was concerned that I might have to drop out. I couldn't tell if I was experiencing jet lag from a recent trip or if I just didn't have the strength. I worried that I had been unrealistic about my fitness for the race. Perhaps I was trying to do too much too soon. Maybe a marathon was too much after all. After the first five miles I began to feel better, and by the halfway mark I knew I would be able to finish. Then I really started to enjoy the run.

The more I ran the stronger I felt. By the time I hit the sixteen-mile mark, I was feeling so good that I started passing other runners. In the last six miles I passed twenty-two racers. The final mile was exhilarating. I felt really strong and healthy for the first time in years.

This was a wonderful moment. At three hours and thirty-three minutes—about eight minutes per mile—this was the slowest marathon I had ever run. But in many ways, it was my greatest running accomplishment. My time was only five minutes slower than my very first Boston Marathon. Only months earlier my health had been at its very lowest point, and I had feared it would degenerate to a level where I would no longer want to live. This race symbolized for me the power of my commitment to heal myself and to live fully.

Another Tragedy

I returned to work after the race with new enthusiasm and energy. The medical practice had grown slowly but steadily since we had opened our office. My nurse Andy and I were an inseparable team. We really enjoyed each other and felt we were building something lasting and valuable. It was Andy who had helped me develop a routine for treating patients when I was blind. I attributed much of my success in being able to continue practicing medicine to her.

Andy was a wonderful person, bubbly and energetic. She was always looking for a way to make things fun. On Halloween she dressed up as a cat with pointy ears, a black leotard, and face paint, and treated patients all day in costume.

Andy dressed up as a cat for Halloween

Andy and I spent so much time together that I felt as close to her as anyone in my life outside of my family. I definitely considered her my best friend in the whole world.

One day at the office that year, Andy told me that she had been feeling depressed and disoriented. We talked about it to see if we could figure out what the problem might be, but we couldn't really identify anything. She liked her work. She was happy in her marriage. Everything in her life was going well.

We made an appointment for the very next morning with a psychiatrist to get an expert's point of view. That night when she dropped me off at home after work, I gave her a big hug and told her how much I loved her and appreciated her.

The next morning Andy didn't come in to work. When she didn't call, I was concerned. Being late and not calling was not at all like her. I called Andy's husband, Gary, at work and told him that I was worried about her. Gary called a neighbor and asked him to check the house while he drove home from work. When Gary got to the house, the neighbor would not let him go in. Andy had shot and killed herself.

I was stunned. How could this have happened to someone like Andy? She was one of the most wonderful people I had ever known. She was kind, energetic, giving, bright, and full of life. Why would she have wanted to kill herself? Ellen and I spent the next several evenings with Gary. We would go for walks together, and Ellen and I would each take one of his arms. We shared our memories of Andy and all the love we had for her. We cried and laughed, and at times just held each other.

Andy had left a suicide note, which I read many times. In the note she was very critical of herself. She said that she was a burden to those around her and that all she did was take from other people. She apologized in the note to all the people that her death would hurt, especially Gary and me. If I had not known Andy's handwriting so well, I would not have believed that she had written it. She was a very giving and generous person, not at all like the person she described in the note.

Such irrational feelings could only have been the result of a depressed mental condition. I started to question whether I was responsible for what had happened to Andy. How could I call myself a good doctor when I hadn't even recognized the symptoms of suicidal depression in my own nurse? I agonized over this and felt very guilty.

Finally, I took the suicide note to a psychiatrist who had experience dealing with suicidal patients. He reassured me that feelings such as those Andy experienced, which are sudden in their onset and totally out of character, have been known to result from brain tumors and brain seizures. Several aspects of Andy's behavior fit the pattern for this type of condition.

Upon further research and medical inquiry, I became convinced that Andy's death almost certainly resulted from brain seizure activity. This helped put to rest my anxiety about having let Andy down by not having prevented a problem that I should have recognized. Andy had always been such a tremendous support in my life that I hated to feel that I had not been there for her when she needed me. I realize now that my guilt was a typical reaction to the suicide of a loved one. I wanted reassurance that I was a good person. I wanted to feel deserving of all the love I felt Andy had given me.

I volunteered to the grieving families to organize and conduct a memorial service. They accepted. We held the service in Andy's and Gary's backyard where their wedding reception had been held one year earlier. During the service I talked about the experiences that Andy and I had shared together and what tremendous love I had for her. I felt so much happiness to have shared in her life that I felt really peaceful. Some of Andy's family and many of her friends also shared their memories and feelings.

After the service people stayed to eat and talk and share with each other. There was a feeling of true celebration of her life. I was able to share with many people all the different emotions that they were experiencing, the grief of their loss, and the joy of their memories.

In talking to Andy's mother after that service, I found that she took antiseizure medicine for temporal lobe seizures. These are the kind of seizures that can cause profound despair. Then I finally knew that Andy probably was also suffering from that same kind of seizure, and that it had not been diagnosed in time.

I had always heard that death is just another part of life. When Andy died, I came to understand that truth in a much deeper way. Initially I had felt a very deep sense of loss and sadness at Andy's death, but by the time of the memorial service I felt considerable acceptance. When I thought about her, I felt happy and close to her.

Then I began to realize that I didn't feel as if I had lost Andy. I felt that she was still very present in my life. The nature of our relationship had changed, that was all. She couldn't help me get patients ready for an examination or give me my elapsed time if we were on a run together, but I still felt that same closeness to her that I had always felt. I still felt that she was supporting me emotionally in the way that she always had. And I still felt that I could share with her in the same way that I always had. The connection that I felt with Andy after her death was stronger than the connection that some people have with the living. Why should I tell myself that I had lost her?

In one sense we have no control over life or physical health. They are gifts that are given to us for a time. We do not gain anything by grieving unrelentingly at their loss. Our only choice is whether or not we will embrace our lives as they are and live them fully. There is great power in this for it is in embracing life fully that we transcend loss and death.

I kept working in my medical practice after Andy's death, and I hired a new nurse, who was excellent, but it was never the same.

11

Searching for Meaning

"Yesterday I was clever, so I wanted to change the world. Today I am wise, so I am changing myself."
—Jelaluddin Rumi

"Australian 9 Day"

I signed up for a personal growth workshop called the "Australian 9 Day" that took place that summer of 1987. This workshop started teaching me lessons before I even left Alaska to fly "down under." For starters, it cost about $3000 for the registration fee. The airfare was an additional $1400. I had never spent that much money on myself before except to buy my 1976 Toyota wagon, brand new for $3600. It was an emotional stretch as well as a financial one for me to spend the money.

I had taken other courses from the Excellerated Learning Institute, and so I decided I'd splurge on myself to attend this course. I thought it would be a great way to further my prosperity consciousness, even if I learned nothing else from the workshop.

The mood was set at the beginning of the workshop. We were going to be pushed to our limit emotionally, physically, and mentally.

The purpose of the stress was simply to force us to get bigger than our problems, to grow in maturity, to be able to expect more from ourselves, and to get outside of our comfort zone so that we could develop a bigger comfort zone.

Class started at 7:00 a.m., and we were directed to quietly write in our journals about what we wanted to get out of the workshop. I remember writing that I wanted to have a transformational experience before the end of the nine days. Next was an exercise period. We were divided into teams and told to start training for an Olympics to be held on the last day of the workshop. We were not told what the Olympic events were going to be. We were just told to get fit!

Many of my team members agreed that we should run to get into good shape and that running was likely to be part of the Olympic competition. Since I had the most experience and expertise with running, I volunteered to coach my team with this part of the training. Another team member led us in stretching exercises and yoga. Another led us through various breathing exercises.

It was really fun for me to take the role of coach for the running exercises. I helped push my team in various games like "leapfrog" running, where the whole team runs single file and the one in last place has to sprint to the front. The leapfrog cycle then repeats until everyone has had the chance to lead the pace.

There were lots of other areas in which to push our limits during the day. On day number 2, the doors to the classroom were locked at exactly 7:00 a.m. A number of people were late and locked out. When the doors were reopened at 7:05 a.m., all those who were late had to stand at the front of class and explain themselves. It was very intimidating.

Our instructor was brilliant and very intense. I think he locked the door to make the point that being late was unacceptable and that "on time" meant "on time," not five minutes late. Holding the people who were late accountable was his way of making all of us more accountable and more responsible for our time, and perhaps more importantly, for keeping our commitment. All of us had agreed that class would start at 7:00 a.m. and that we would be there, and yet he needed to teach that lesson more dramatically on day 2 because apparently not everyone had his same understanding of time.

I wasn't even one of the late ones, but I vowed to make sure I would be even a little earlier the rest of the week. I didn't want to have to face being called onto the carpet and embarrassed in front of the whole class. It gave me a deeper awareness of keeping my time agreements.

Another nerve-racking activity developed from the assignment that each of us would have to sing a song in front of our classmates. Everyone was given a tape from which to learn the song. We all got different songs. One side of the tape held both the music and the recorded song with words. The other side was just the instrumental version. During the day at unpredictable times, the instructor would take a break from the lecture material and call out a few names of people whose turn it was to sing. The suspense and anxiety nearly killed me.

My song was Elvis Presley's "Don't Be Cruel." When it came my turn, I had to do the singing to the music-only side of my tape. I didn't get to sing along with Elvis. I was shaking like a leaf—not like Elvis—by the time I was into the second verse. I was still shaking thirty minutes afterward.

Later I realized how much of a stretch that Elvis number had been for me. Speaking in front of a group or sharing my opinions would never again seem very scary by comparison. I was really relieved when I was finally done with my turn, and I enjoyed the other classmates' performances so much more throughout the week because my nervousness was gone.

As the end of the workshop approached, I felt like I had learned a lot about myself. I learned about the way I processed new information. I learned about some of my beliefs that were no longer serving me. For example, I realized that I could no longer be casual about keeping my time commitment, and from that day on, I have always been on time.

Our instructor adhered to a personal philosophy of "perturbation," a belief that people won't change unless they are shaken from their complacency. He intentionally forced us to reexamine and change our ideas, beliefs, and behaviors. I was frequently pushed outside of my comfort zone.

I also had developed some very significant friendships with my fellow classmates and particularly with my exercise team members. I felt that the whole week had been extremely valuable for me in countless ways. I also felt like I hadn't really had a significant transformational experience. I hadn't yet experienced what I had come to get.

A Team Transformation

For our Olympics, we lined up in our teams and marched around a playing field just like in the opening ceremony for the real Olympics. It felt a little corny, but it certainly was exciting.

As our instructor began explaining the rules, each team was given a raw egg to carry throughout all the events. If any team broke their egg, they were eliminated from the competition. Each of the 125 participants in the workshop also put in $10.00 to create a $1250.00 prize for the winning team. The stakes were high.

There were five team events. In the first one, we had to lie down on the playing field, shoulder to shoulder with our teammates. We then took turns being lifted up and over the team, in leapfrog fashion, so that the team moved slowly down the field. If a player got dropped, he or she had to go back to the beginning of their team's line and get passed along again. Each team had to protect the precious raw egg. It was fun, and a good warm-up exercise.

As the games unfolded, the events became tougher. In the fourth event, the team had to run together holding hands for about one-half mile uphill, and the team was not finished until all members crossed the finish line. Our team won that event, and it looked like all our running practice was paying off.

As we gathered for the final event, it was apparent that only my team and one other were in real contention for first place. The pressure was really on.

The final event turned out to be a relay race involving the best two runners from each team. One runner from the team would start on top of a hill about one-half mile from the playing field where we were all huddled. At the bottom, he would tag the second runner, who would run up the hill and back down. Since I had been coaching my team in running all week, they wanted me to be one of our two representative runners, and I decided to do the second and longer leg. Our first runner went to his starting position with the egg, and we all assumed it would be handed to me like a baton when it was my turn to run.

After the first runners were gone, we were all told that the rules had changed. The first runners had been instructed to hide the egg somewhere up on top of the hill. So, good communication became part of the handoff. The second runner would have to find his team's egg before running downhill to the finish line. Each egg had the team's number painted on it for identification.

I immediately got concerned. With my level of visual impairment, I was afraid I might get lost just trying to follow the dirt path to the top of the hill. I was supposed to turn into the woods after passing a broken down, old, white school bus in the woods. I wasn't even sure I would be able to spot the white school bus. I hadn't noticed it all week, so finding the egg seemed impossible for me.

My teammates insisted that I be their runner despite my protestations. They said I was their best hope. Although I had told them my fears, I couldn't change their minds. If I could find my way past the old bus, I thought I still might be able to win this race and the $1250.00 for my team. I can't remember being more nervous before a race, and I had run hundreds of them since my school days.

Once my teammate touched my hand and gave me directions to find our egg, I took off as fast as I could. My lungs were burning, my legs aching, and my body quivering with exertion by the time I found the old white bus and turned into the woods and up the final hill.

When I got to the hilltop, there were a few other competitors hunting for their eggs, but no one had started toward home yet. Time ground to a standstill for me as I unsuccessfully searched for my team's egg. Just as I had feared, I could not locate it. My vision was just too poor.

After several minutes, all of my competitors had found their team's egg and headed off down the hill. I was flat-footed, forlorn, and overcome with disappointment. After about four minutes had elapsed, I knew all the other runners would have finished, and I still didn't have the egg. Finally, recognizing my handicap problem, one of the assistants supervising the race led me to the little white orb.

At that instant, I made a momentous decision. I wouldn't let my visual impairment stop me from participating fully in this race. I would run as fast as I could even though I had no chance of winning.

As I sped down the hill, my heart pounded, and I sprinted as fast as I could go. It was both exhilarating and frightening at the same time. I was a little worried that I wouldn't see a rock or log and would end up tripping if I ran too fast. I chose to go fast anyway. I wouldn't let my vision stop me.

As I reached the final 200 yards to the finish line, I could hear all 124 classmates cheering me onward. My eyes clouded over from sheer exertion. I felt as if I were running through a narrow tunnel, through a foggy cloud. I lost all peripheral vision.

As I raced toward the finish, an onlooker jumped into stride next to me for the final fifty yards. He told me later that he had felt compelled to run with me. He said he had a strange sensation that he must run beside me. I was relieved when he joined me, realizing that at least someone would see where I was going.

By the time we crossed the finish line, I was nearly blind from exhaustion, and overcome with emotion and tears. I knew I had run my hardest. I started to try to apologize to my teammates, but they wouldn't hear any of it. They lifted me up onto their shoulders like a champion. I was totally overwhelmed with their acceptance and praise. I wept with joy.

Later that day I realized that that run had been my transformational experience. I had transcended the limitation of my poor vision. I had learned how to play life at 100 percent, full tilt, no holding back, despite my vision.

I was rewarded with a new and deeper appreciation of my own worth, and greater self-acceptance and self-respect. I felt as though in that moment of running through a tunnel of fog, I had felt the hand of God guiding me safely to the finish. Perhaps it was also God's will that the other runner guided me through the last fifty yards in my exhaustion. My prayer for a transformational experience had been answered.

12

Watching the River Run

> *And it goes on and on, watching the river run,*
> *Further and further from things that we've done,*
> *Leaving them one by one.*
> *And we have just begun watching the river run.*
> *Listening, learning and yearning*
> *Run river run.*
> —Loggins & Messina, "Watching the River Run"

About the time I began dating Ellen, I realized for the first time that I was ready for and wanted a single, committed, lifelong relationship. As I spent time with Ellen, I fell more and more in love with her, and I began to want that lifelong relationship with her.

There was a hitch, however. She was not sure she wanted me as a lifelong partner. She was straightforward about her doubts, and this was very hard for me to hear.

I thought about why this was so hard, and I decided that perhaps it was because her doubts about marrying me reinforced my own doubts about myself. Deep down, I had always questioned whether I was a worthy mate. I had wondered whether it was fair to ask anyone to marry me given that I might have a shorter than average lifespan or serious health complications or that I might pass on imperfect genes to my children.

Rationally, these doubts did not make sense. Nothing was guaranteed in Ellen's life any more than in mine. Ellen might have a short life or debilitating illness or imperfect genes, yet it didn't deter my wish to be with her. But my doubts about my own worthiness seemed to speak louder than my logic. Noticing how strong this self-doubt was, I realized that Ellen was not likely to have much faith in our life together if I didn't have faith in it.

I finally decided that perhaps the best thing I could do for my relationship with Ellen was to improve my relationship with myself—to start supporting and appreciating myself and changing the negative views I had about my own worthiness. To do this, I began just to notice any feelings of inadequacy, doubt, or sadness whenever they came up. I could usually trace feeling "bad" to a situation or conversation where I felt doubts about whether I was worthwhile or good. Then without reproaching myself for either the feelings or the thought, I would gently rephrase the self-doubt to reflect faith in myself and my value. I forgave myself freely for mistakes that I might have previously derided myself for.

I was learning to become my own best friend. I found that kindness and love for myself gave rise to feelings of kindness and love for other people. It was the opposite of the "vicious cycle." It was a cycle of kindness and support that affected others as well as myself. It made me feel happier and less in need of Ellen's approval. Interestingly, when I needed Ellen's approval less, she had more to give.

From time to time I would find a quiet place, meditate, and reflect on whether things would work out for us. I would always get the feeling that they would, but not until Ellen was ready.

I would talk with Ellen sometimes about my old fears of unworthiness and my shifting beliefs. I was feeling worthy of the best that life had to offer, including a good marriage. I was realizing that quality of life has nothing to do with longevity. Ellen gradually warmed to the idea that ten or fifteen happy and fulfilling years with someone you love was worthwhile.

On several occasions during the next year, I thought Ellen was finally ready to commit to marriage. Each time I was hit hard by the realization that I was seeing what I wanted to see rather than what she was feeling. As upsetting as this was each time, I would eventually remember that I could love her whether or not she loved me, and I could love myself regardless of what she did.

I finally got to the point where I felt enough inner support for myself that my doubts about my worthiness totally dissipated. I even began to feel grateful for Ellen's resistance

because it had pushed me to learn greater acceptance for myself. I also began to find that my love for myself and my love for Ellen were inseparable. Sometime during the second year of our courtship she decided that she did want to marry me.

Ellen and I were married on June 21, 1988, the summer solstice. The beautiful ceremony took place at a scenic mountain lodge on the tundra-covered slopes of the Chugach Range.

After we were married, Ellen and I enjoyed overnight backpacking in the Alaskan wilderness.

As a wedding present we were given a sleek sea kayak "built for two" with which to explore Alaska's rugged coastline together. Warmed by the evening sun and the love of friends, I felt very happy to be alive.

My marriage to Ellen launched me into a period not only of happiness but also of major adjustments. Ellen had two children from a previous marriage, Kerry, six years old, and Christopher, eight years old. They quickly shook up all of my little routines.

Ellen, whitewater rafting (but not in our kayak)

Ellen and I were married June 21, 1988. Kerry was six, and Christopher was eight.

When I would pull out the tasty snacks I carried for my hypoglycemia, for example, I would find that everyone else suddenly had low blood sugar too. I was not always easily convinced to pass them around.

It was interesting to spend my workday acting the part of the mature, wise doctor/counselor, and then come home and have to argue with the children. One thing maturation had given me, however, was plenty of experience in looking at upsets as opportunities for resolution and growth. An easy solution to the diminishing snack problem was simply to start packing more snacks.

Making these adjustments was tremendously rewarding. Having had to adjust to losing my sight and good health had reaffirmed for me how precious each day of health is. I think this perception also rubbed off on Ellen as she had to adjust to my tendency not to put off my enjoyment or rewards.

We celebrated our health and the beauty of our surroundings with frequent kayaking, hiking, and camping trips. We also enjoyed regular visits from my mom and brother Stephen, who were eager to experience Alaska's scenery and incredible outdoor activities for themselves.

Kenny and I with Mom on a rare picture-perfect day at Denali National Park with Mt. Denali behind us

Kenny and Stephen enjoying the hot tub, a popular Alaskan indulgence following strenuous outdoor activities

Open My Eyes: A Doctor's Powerful Story of Courage & Healing

Above: I dressed appropriately for a July hike in Alaska to reach a snowfield for summer skiing, wearing a warm hat and jacket.

Left: Once at the snowfield, where the temperature was warmed by the sun reflecting off the snow, I could strip down to my pink and blue Farlander running shorts for a glorious and comfortable afternoon of summer skiing.

Four Women

As my health continued to improve and I returned to marathoning, I began getting invitations to speak to various groups about diabetes and about healing. In some cases, I was able to combine speaking with running, and Ellen was able to travel with me.

As I traveled and spoke, I was surprised to find that people with diabetes often knew very little about the disease.

At one seminar a woman expressed frustration at her consistently high blood sugar levels. I asked her if she was on a special diet that would help to keep her blood sugar down. She answered that she didn't realize a special diet was necessary.

At another seminar for people with diabetes, a woman responded to some comments I made about human and animal insulin by saying she hadn't even known human insulin was available.

(Although the first insulin developed for diabetes treatment came from the pancreas of pigs and cattle, human insulin produced by

Portland Marathon, 1989

Above: With Ellen and our friend Suzy after the race
Below: Me running the marathon

using a novel lab technique came on the market in the mid-1980s. Today, almost all insulin used in the U.S. is human insulin.)

To me this was like finding a person who had not heard that we'd landed on the moon. I was struck by how much I could raise people's awareness just by talking about the basics of good health, like eating well and getting exercise.

In 1989, I gave a talk in Ketchikan, a fishing town in Southeast Alaska that was enjoying a streak of unseasonably sunny, warm weather. Southeast Alaskans learn to take advantage of those rare days to be outside if at all possible, so it didn't surprise me that only four people showed up for my presentation.

"Is there more you are willing to do to feel better?"

Self-healing is a topic I always discussed as a guest speaker.

Seeing this as an opportunity to connect on a very personal level, I arranged our chairs in a circle, and the five of us sat and talked. One of those in attendance was a woman who had heard me speak two years earlier. She could not seem to get over how much healthier and more vibrant I looked.

I was pleased at her observation because one of the points I wanted to make to this group was the simple truth that we are capable of making changes and becoming healthier and happier. She could see that I had made changes in my life; she seemed to realize she could do the same.

Before the seminar was over, the four participants were exchanging phone numbers, making agreements to exercise together, and enjoying a real bond that had been established. As I hugged each of them goodbye, I wondered whether the bond of affection and friendship that had been established in the seminar was just as important or even more important than anything I had said.

Two months after the seminar, I received a letter from the woman who had commented on my appearance. She thanked me for giving the seminar and said that in only two months she'd lost thirty pounds. She went on to say that she'd brought her blood sugar and blood pressure under better control, and she indicated that she was feeling happier and less stressed. A subtle shift in attitude can be the precursor of great change and happiness.

My seminars did not always evoke a warm response, however. A few months later, at a seminar in Seattle during a question-and-answer session, I was faced with some very hostile, angry questions from a couple in the audience. This man and woman had been a professional dance team until the woman began to have problems with neuropathy, or nerve damage, from her diabetes. She was having difficulty with her balance and was unable to do extensive workouts as she had in the past. They were clearly angry about what was happening, and angry at me. Perhaps they felt that I was a charlatan offering false hope.

But as I listened to them, I initially wondered if I would feel threatened by their hostility. As I listened further, I felt complimented that they felt safe enough with me to express their anger and raise hard questions. They concluded by saying that their doctors had told them that there was nothing they could do about her neuropathy.

Expressing appreciation for their forthrightness, I answered that I believed there were always things a person could do to improve his or her health. I mentioned studies that indicated that good diabetic control could not only limit the progression of neuropathy and keep it from getting worse but could actually improve the symptoms.

After the question-and-answer session, the couple came up and expressed their gratitude for my presentation. I could see that something had shifted or changed in them, and I felt delighted. This experience reinforced for me the importance of letting people know that little if anything is absolute, and that life is full of different approaches and possibilities.

This experience also helped me realize that just accepting people could help get my message across. Perhaps this couple just needed to express their anger in an atmosphere of acceptance before they could work on solving their problem.

Although I was acting as a teacher in these seminars, I often found myself in the position of the student. During one seminar I mentioned that the average lifespan of a person with type 1 diabetes was 32 years.

"I don't intend to go along with that statistic," I said, intending to stir up some life and fight in the group. "I'm 39 now, and going for 64," I concluded, and paused to check out the reaction.

"Would you like to have more energy?"

From the back of the room came a voice asking me why I didn't set my sights a little higher. The voice belonged to an 84-year-old woman who had been a diabetic for fifty years.

Experiences like this have convinced me that we really grow by helping each other. My own experiences with healing are not out of the ordinary in terms of what others have done nor what we are all capable of. We each have a deep well of natural humor, love, wisdom, and experience to share. Life is about learning to tap into that well.

A Leap of Faith

During the time after Andy's death and in the first two years of my marriage, my vision stabilized at around the 20/60 level in my one seeing eye, my right. This was certainly excellent vision compared to total blindness.

Unfortunately, I grew increasingly impatient with taking taxis back and forth to work because I couldn't drive a car. It was particularly aggravating to get off work at around 5:00 p.m. and then have to wait thirty to forty-five minutes for a taxi. I lived only three miles from the Providence Hospital where my office was located. At 5:00 p.m., however, the cab company had its change of shifts, and I would invariably have a long wait.

In fact, I could have walked home in the time it took to wait for a taxi, but in Anchorage during winter that was impractical due to the four to six feet of snow berms that completely covered any sidewalk. I recognized that I had quite a transportation issue. Once I started calling it an issue, I realized I could investigate potential solutions.

My eye doctor had identified that I had developed a cataract in my right eye. I decided to check out the possibility of having the cataract removed. The cataract surgeon I saw advised that he thought my vision could improve significantly with the surgery, possibly even to the 20/40 level. This was important, as the 20/40 level on the eye chart is the driving line.

I was initially quite heartened. However, he cautioned that sometimes the surgery goes poorly. At the time, cataract surgery was considered elective surgery and not required; the risk was real. Today's ophthalmologists routinely perform this surgery with significantly less risk of serious side effects.

I was told that if I developed one of many possible complications, I might go totally blind again, but this time permanently. He also started referring to me as a "one-eyed man," which I found both rude and very disconcerting.

"If you develop any sign of a cold or flu-bug, we'll postpone the surgery," he said. "We don't want to take any unnecessary risks in a one-eyed man."

It took some hard looking within for me to decide to have this surgery. I realized that I really wanted to start driving again. I had driven from age sixteen to age thirty-four before my eyesight had failed me. It had been six years of waiting on buses and taxis that had brought me to the brink of this surgery.

A question I had often asked attendees at my seminars is a question I now asked myself.

"What are you willing to do to change your life?"

I also realized that there were real risks involved, and I really didn't want to be blind again. I didn't think I could live with the idea that I had brought on permanent blindness just because of being impatient with public transportation. It wasn't worth it, even if I did have to waste time waiting for taxis and buses.

I decided to start using the tools I had learned while I was blind. I started affirming, "I am safe to have surgery."

I also started visualizing myself coming through the surgery with no problems. Turning within using meditation, I quietly reflected on my choice. Finally, I came to believe that I could undergo the cataract surgery without fear of complications.

About that time, a friend gave me the quote from Patrick Overton that strengthened my courage. I knew then for certain that if I took this step into the darkness of the unknown, there would either be something solid to stand on, or I would be taught how to fly.

In July 1990, one week after my fortieth birthday, I had cataract surgery. It happened without a hitch. I had to endure twenty-four hours of blindness due to my bandaged eyes. My white cane came out for the first time in more than four years, and I remembered how frightening blindness had been.

Once the bandages were off, I could see 20/40. A month later I got my Alaska driver's license! I did roll into one stop sign while practicing for that driver's test, but only my ego was dented. A week after being licensed, I bought myself a car and started waving at taxis and buses as I drove myself back and forth to work.

13

Ocean Kayaking

"The best thing about Anchorage is that it's only 10 minutes from Alaska."
—A popular saying among those wanting to get out into the wilderness

When I lived in Anchorage, the average age was twenty-six years old, and nearly everyone loved to go camping, river rafting, kayaking, glacier hopping, mountain climbing, backpacking, fishing, or whatever else would get them out of the city and into the wilderness.

Ellen and I were no exception. We used our free time to relax, celebrate the outdoors, and get some exercise. The boundless opportunities to enjoy a healthy lifestyle was, in fact, a primary reason I had moved to Alaska.

Harrison Fiord is one of those pristine, wilderness seascapes in Alaska, off the beaten track. I had a glorious kayaking trip there in 1991 with Ellen, my brother Kenny, and his bride-to-be, Diane. Diane's parents, Bill and Carol, joined the expedition along with Tim and his wife, Cathy, who were visiting from Wisconsin. Bill and Carol combined this kayaking trip with the celebration of Kenny and Diane's wedding. Ellen and I took about three of these trips each summer, and this one was typically memorable.

Harrison Fjord is about a three-hour charter boat ride out of Whittier, Alaska, in a remote part of Prince William Sound. As is frequently the case, the tip of the fjord is marked by a large glacier, in this case named Harrison Glacier. We camped all five days on a small beach about three miles from the glacier. There were three different glaciers that touched the water's edge on the fjord, all within easy paddling distance from our base camp. Each morning, after a robust breakfast and camp coffee, all eight of us would pile into our ocean-going kayaks and head off paddling to one of the three glaciers. The scenery was spectacular. As we would get close to a glacier, about three-quarters of a mile, we could hear and see the ice calving into the sea. We couldn't get closer than about one-half mile without the risk of being swamped by a wave from the calving glacier.

The small icebergs would also start getting so thick in the water around the kayak that they would prevent traveling any closer. The kayaks were seaworthy but made of lightweight fiberglass. It would have been very easy to puncture the hull if rammed by even the smallest hunk of ice. Because the water was only about 34 degrees near the glacier, even in summer, it was imperative not to take undue risks in those tiny boats. Capsizing or sinking would quickly have become life-endangering because one would become hypothermic in less than five minutes. In just those few minutes, it would have become impossible to swim or pull oneself up out of the water into a kayak. We always gave the glaciers and icebergs plenty of room.

The water teemed with sea animals. Every day we would see some playful otters floating on their backs nearby. We also frequently saw seals, who more shyly kept their distance. On this particular trip, we were delighted to see a pair of Orca whales come swimming by our camp. They were feeding on their way up toward the glacier, less than one-hundred yards offshore.

In that part of Alaska in midsummer, it stays light until midnight, so there is a whole afternoon worth of light remaining after 6:00 p.m. In camp, we would have hours of quality visiting time in the evening after supper. Bill and Carol were both lawyers in their sixties from Los Angeles. Kenny and Diane were also both lawyers but in their thirties. It was fun for me to hear so much legal discussion and political commentary. Tim was an experienced kayaker and outdoor adventurer. He was quite at ease in the Alaskan wilderness. Cathy was a lot less experienced but no less enthusiastic. She joined in on every outing.

Ellen and I owned a double kayak Tofino, which was given to us as a wedding present three years earlier by all of our friends. It was a Cadillac of a boat, twenty-three feet long, and custom painted pink and blue.

It became a standing joke that in most of the kayaking pictures of the two of us, she is in the front seat paddling, and I am in the back seat eating. My excuse was that Alaska was such a physically demanding country that I had to eat all day long. I did, however, manage to see some beautiful scenery and incredible wildlife—whales, seals, and sea otters—in between snacks.

With my visual impairment, I would have been anxious about getting separated from the others and lost at sea in a small single-person kayak. In the double kayak, I could count on Ellen's good vision to keep us from getting lost. She could count on my strong arms and back to power us along wherever we decided to go. We made a good team.

On one excursion we were all heading back to camp when we decided to practice "precision paddling." We pretended to be like a marching band, and all lifted our paddles synchronously, paddling in precise rhythm. It was really fun to demonstrate our art when the sightseeing boat, filled with tourists, would pass near us on its daily voyage back to Whittier. I still wonder if some of those visiting gawkers thought that all kayaking was done in rhythm like the rowing of a crew team.

Taking care of my diabetes in this type of adventure took a little extra attention. I had to make sure my insulin wouldn't freeze, so I kept it in an insulated case. Constant paddling for hours at a time also burned up a lot of calories. To prevent hypoglycemia, I had to keep eating at regular intervals.

I usually settled on gorp, a rich mixture of "good ol' raisins and peanuts," with some added M&M's® for extra sugar. I also kept some ropes of black licorice for fuel for the last hour of paddling back to camp.

In general, everyone was pretty tired by the end of a long day of paddling. I certainly was as tired as anyone. The difference between me and the others was that I couldn't allow myself to get too hypoglycemic if there was still paddling to do. If I had ever run low on blood sugar and run out of my emergency rations of gorp or licorice, I would have been in real trouble. Paddling for another fifteen minutes to reach camp would have been impossible in that instance. To be safe, I always made sure I had plenty of sweet, high-energy foods.

For some reason, Ellen seemed to need extra food for energy at about the same time as I would. Since I didn't want to be selfish, I learned to carry along enough goodies for both of us.

In those early years of our marriage, I don't think Ellen really believed that my being out of "emergency rations," as I called them, was actually a dangerous situation for me. I think she thought that I just had a sweet tooth. However, the threat of rapid onset of life-threatening hypoglycemic shock was very real. I somehow managed to share my licorice and never got dangerously hypoglycemic.

When we got back to Anchorage after five days of kayaking, Kenny and Diane were married with all of us in attendance. In Alaska, anyone could apply to be the marriage minister, and Ellen performed the ceremony. No one smelled of campfire smoke or sea salt. It was great to be back on dry land in dry clothes.

With Ellen in our double kayak in Alaska, where I am uncharacteristically paddling instead of snacking.

14

The Sunny Southwest

For there is a new world to be won—a world of peace and good will, a world of hope and abundance.
—John F. Kennedy, Televised press conference, July 4, 1960

That summer of 1991, Ellen and I decided to move to Arizona. Ellen's parents and sisters lived there, and we wanted to live in a warmer and sunnier locale. We certainly found it in Prescott. In the heat of summer, it can reach 100 degrees but usually doesn't go higher than 95 degrees. Prescott is at 5300 feet elevation and is consistently 20 degrees cooler than Phoenix. In the winter, the temperature drops below freezing many nights but will soar to 50 degrees in the warmest part of the afternoon.

Prescott's population then was about 35,000 people. Although it's grown significantly, Prescott is still a wonderful community. It was almost impossible to go downtown to shop or dine at a restaurant without seeing one or more of my friends. I liked that. I got a strong sense of community, and I liked the small-town atmosphere, friendliness, and the peacefully slow pace of life in the Arizona Highlands.

The first Sunday that Ellen and I were in Prescott, we decided to check out a local church service. We picked the Unity Church of Prescott. It felt like home from that first visit, especially since that day we met four or five people who had previously lived in Anchorage. We became regular Sunday churchgoers and began to volunteer. Ellen took on the challenge of co-coordinating the Sunday music program, singing and playing music about every other week. Within a few years I was elected as president of the Unity Board of Directors. The minister, Rev. Tom, and his wife, Pam, became our closest friends.

My New Family Practice in Prescott

Each morning I awakened at 6:50 a.m. to my wristwatch alarm. It was a talking watch. I was given my first talking watch by my mother in 1984, the Christmas that I was blind. "It's 6:50 a.m., please hurry up." My watch's digital-doll, female voice harkened. I would enjoy a five-minute snooze before she reminded me again, "It's 6:55 a.m., please hurry up." Sometimes I snoozed a second time, then I was shower-bound and getting ready for work.

I left for work at 8:00 a.m. My medical office was small and cozy, and I was my own boss. An easy commute, it was only 2.2 miles from my home. I would have ridden my bicycle if there had been a bike path. As it was, I drove a teal, four-cylinder sedan 1992 Mercedes Benz, the smallest and least expensive Mercedes made. I leased it in May 1992 as a way of stretching my mind into a more prosperous consciousness. It worked! I felt abundant driving that little car. I felt successful and continued to feel thankful that I could see well enough to drive at all.

On a typical day, I would see sixteen to twenty-two patients in my office. I nearly always kept my schedule on time so that no one had to wait more than fifteen minutes from their appointment time. I felt it was disrespectful to my patients to have them wait. I learned how terrible that was when I had to wait during those long spells before my laser treatments.

As much as possible, I spent time educating my patients. In a typical office visit, I would discuss the factors leading up to or contributing to the illness at hand. I then outlined the steps to be taken to get well and emphasized the rationale for each step. Finally, I discussed how to prevent this illness from happening again.

Let's say, for example, that a woman had symptoms of a urinary tract infection, which was a common situation in my practice. In taking her history, I would ask how often during the day she normally urinated, and how much water or other fluids she drank. If she didn't drink much liquid, she may have had to void only once or twice during a workday.

I pointed out that there were always bacteria around that could travel up the urethra and lead to a bladder infection. I also explained that bacteria could reproduce in about twenty minutes. If the bacteria doubled every twenty minutes, there would be eight-fold as many after one hour. The best natural defense a woman had to prevent infection was to drink more fluids and to void regularly, like every few hours. Voiding washed the bacteria out of the bladder.

Additionally, I emphasized the importance of going when the first urge hits. If my patient waited a whole hour to use the restroom, there would be many more bacteria trying to start an infection. Also, the overstretched bladder wall wouldn't get adequate blood flow and would be more susceptible to infection. So I stressed ways to keep the infection from recurring. I got great satisfaction in helping people take better care of themselves.

Because of my interest and personal experience with diabetes, I saw a lot of patients with diabetes in my practice. The most common topics I discussed were weight reduction, dietary modification, how to start and stick to an exercise program, how to stop smoking, how to improve blood glucose control to decrease the complications of diabetes, and how to feel better in one's life despite the hurdles. I limited the number of people I scheduled in any one day so that I had time for all this educating and counseling.

The benefit to me was that I felt I was making a big difference in my patients' lives. I was fulfilled and satisfied in my work. Most people really appreciated the fact that I took the time to answer all their questions. Of course, when I took the extra time to address both the physical and emotional needs of my patients, I often heard from them how much they appreciated my spending the extra time, so I felt appreciated. It was a good exchange.

I worked about forty hours a week, which was a pretty light schedule compared to most doctors. I learned long ago how damaging too much stress could be to my well-being. My goal was to stay as healthy and happy as I could, so I carefully monitored what stresses I would allow in my life. Work stress was not something I could safely ignore.

15

A Picture of Health

> *Good health is having no fatigue; having a good appetite; going to sleep and awakening easily; having a good memory; having good humor; having precision in thought and action; and being honest, humble, grateful, and loving.*
> —Louise Hay, *You Can Heal Your Life*, Hay House LLC, 1984

I ran the Los Angeles Marathon in March 1992. It was a wonderful marathon for a lot of reasons. The training I had done leading up to the race was relatively easy, enjoyable, and rewarding. Much of my training was shared with my nurse friend, Ruth Ann. Months before race day, we decided to run the race together. That decision took away a lot of the pressure from me. It was my thirty-first marathon. It was Ruth Ann's third. Her goal was to improve on her previous best time of three hours forty-five minutes. My goal was simply to have the whole experience be as joyful as possible.

Her goal time would not be too hard for me. My training involved working up to about fifty miles per week for the ten weeks prior to race day. I didn't have any significant injuries plaguing me in the final weeks leading up to the race. Running with Ruth Ann made the long runs of fifteen to eighteen miles go a lot easier. I would sometimes forget I was on a two-hour run because of our interesting conversations.

One of the really special aspects of this race was that it was held in my brother Stephen's hometown, and he was planning to run the race. This would be his first marathon since 1973 when he unofficially entered the Boston Marathon. He had never trained for that race, or even planned to run it. With all the excitement at the starting point in Hopkington, Massachusetts, he somehow was talked into running the first five-mile segment. Our brother Kenny was planning to hand me a sugar bottle every five miles along the racecourse. The plan was that Stephen could drop out of the race after running five miles and then ride to Boston in the car with Kenny and help pass me my sugar bottles. We agreed that Stephen would then have had the excitement and fun of participating in this great running event. After all, a five-mile run wouldn't be too difficult.

Once the race started, I never saw Stephen again, as I was well-trained and a fast runner. The traffic was so heavy, however, that Kenny barely reached the designated five-mile mark in the car before I came running along looking for my sugar bottle. He knew that getting my bottles was of paramount importance in my performance. He knew that if he waited for Stephen to come along, he would likely miss me at the ten-mile mark. Fortunately for me, he decided to speed on to the next checkpoint.

Stephen, Mom, and I celebrate Stephen's first 10K race at Weeona Lake, many years prior to his 1992 Los Angeles marathon.

Unfortunately for Stephen, there was no Kenny to pick him up at five miles. Stephen decided he would have to hope to meet Kenny at the ten-mile mark. With the heavy traffic, Kenny continued to barely get to the checkpoints before I did, and never could wait for Stephen. Stephen continued to find no Kenny, no car to collapse into, and no way to get back to Boston except on foot.

He told us later that he couldn't even stop to walk without getting an embarrassing boost of encouraging remarks from the throngs of spectators. They shouted to him to keep going, and he felt a fair amount of guilt for walking.

The problem was, Stephen had not done any marathon training. He had done scarcely any running in the four years that had elapsed since his high school cross-country days. I finished that Boston Marathon in two hours and fifty-eight minutes. It was a very respectable time for me and under seven minutes per mile for the entire race. When I found Kenny at the Prudential Center in downtown Boston after the race, he told me about not being able to wait for Stephen. We both figured Stephen would probably have hitchhiked a ride to Boston.

Relaxing at the finish chute area, Kenny and I watched runners struggle up the last hill to the finish line. At three hours and fifty-eight minutes on the big digital clock positioned at the finish line, I suddenly was astonished to see Stephen. He was still running—half running and half dragging himself—toward the finish. I couldn't believe it! He had run the Boston Marathon without training and finished in just under four hours. It was incredible!

We were so overwhelmed and overjoyed with his accomplishment that he couldn't bring himself to tell us that he had taken a ride in a car for about one-half mile out on the course. We were so full of praise that he was too embarrassed to tell us he didn't really run the whole marathon. In truth, his accomplishment was no less incredible if he had only run twenty-five miles rather than the full marathon distance.

I thought about the Greek soldier, Pheidippides, who ran the first marathon from the Plains of Marathon to Athens, Greece, 26.2 miles. His message was to announce the victory of the Athenian army over the invading Persians. As the legend goes, that runner died on the steps of the palace after uttering, "We have conquered."

Stephen really had conquered and survived in his debut marathon effort that day in 1973. Now, nineteen years later, his plan was to run the entire Los Angeles Marathon without any lifts in a car. He planned to clear up this deception and secret he had held for so many years. He wanted to be able to say he had truly run a marathon and not have to think that he might have cheated a little.

Ruth Ann and I ran the Los Angeles marathon together.

When the race in L.A. finally unfolded, Stephen realized his dream. He again ran around four hours, but every step was under his own power, and his months of training had paid off. He was also a lot less sore than he had been nineteen years earlier in Boston.

Ruth Ann made her goal and ran the race in three hours forty-three minutes. We ran every step together. We even picked up the pace for the final one-and-a-half miles to make sure she would attain her best time ever.

I counted fifty-two live musical acts along the 26.2-mile course. There were also an uncountable number of people in costumes, dancers, cheering fans, and gaping onlookers. It was a carnival atmosphere for me. I also reached my goal that day. I had the most fun I had ever had in running a marathon.

16

My Sore Foot

Faith has to do with things that are not seen, and hope with things that are not in hand.
—Saint Thomas Aquinas, *Summa Theologica*

After returning home to Prescott, I settled back into a routine of running about thirty-five miles a week. I wasn't doing any really difficult training, and no other races were planned. I was simply enjoying being able to go out for a five-mile run after work along the trails of the Prescott National Forest, adjacent to the subdivision where I lived.

In September 1992, I traveled to Singapore and Australia for a one-month speaking tour.

I'd been invited to Singapore by the Diabetes Society of Singapore to speak at their 21st anniversary meeting. It was an absolutely wonderful week. I was wined and dined like visiting royalty by the many doctors who were officers and board members of the Society.

In addition to my presentations, I did every possible tourist thing I could manage. One day I took a guided bus tour to see all the highlights of the city. Another day I went to the zoo. On another memorable day, I visited the Tang Dynasty City theme park, which included dinner and entertainment that featured singing and dancing from an early period considered to be a golden age of Chinese arts and culture. It was spectacular!

After six days in Singapore, I flew to Australia for a full three-week tour. In that period, I gave five evening presentations and three full-day workshops on self-healing. My stops included Perth, Melbourne, Adelaide, and Sydney, and I enjoyed around five days in each city. I also did what felt like countless radio interviews and breakfast club talks to promote my tour. One really fun day in Sydney included a guest appearance on "Good Morning Australia."

I made a point of taking a good run each day to help manage the stress of so many speaking engagements, meeting so many new people, and the rigorous travel schedule. I reasoned that if I could go out and have a relaxing run, I could manage all the stress that was put in front of me.

As extra protection against all the stress, I decided to have a massage in each of the four cities I visited. That definitely seemed to help. An interesting thing I discovered about therapeutic massage in Australia is that it is customary to have no sheet or towel as draping. Another shock to me was that the massage therapist didn't leave the room as I started to get undressed. In all four cities, they simply kept talking to me as I undressed and climbed up onto the table.

I accepted that this sort of custom could be expected to vary in different parts of the world. It just caught me a little off guard. In America, when I would have a massage, the massage therapist would always leave the room while I undressed and positioned myself on the table under a sheet or towel.

I had the same sort of shocked reaction when I discovered that women in Australia would sunbathe and swim topless at the beaches if they chose to, even in suburban Sydney.

Adelaide was my third Australian city on the tour, and by then I was already feeling the strain of my busy schedule and daily appointments with the media. In Adelaide, I made one television talk show appearance in addition to three different radio station interviews.

While I was there, I stayed with Phillip and Jan, friends whom I had met years earlier. Phillip had participated in the Australian nine-day workshop with me in 1987. Phillip and Jan lived in a wonderful beach house. To go for a run, I simply walked out their back door to the clean, sandy beach.

As a coping strategy, I boosted my running to twice a day for the four days I was living on the beach. It felt heavenly to run along the hard sand at the ocean's edge. My tension would drain away like the retreating water after each crashing wave.

My evening talk and full-day workshops went well in Adelaide. There were fewer participants than hoped for, but I was well-received. I certainly felt successful and accomplished.

The final few days in Australia were spent in Sydney where I stayed with my good friends Joe and Dee. I had known them since 1979 when they lived in Lancaster, Kentucky. Joe was a dentist and Dee his dental hygienist, and together they had operated one of only three dental offices in the area.

We had become the closest of friends while I was working as one of four doctors in that small rural community. That was the period of highest stress and most overwork in my life. In those days in Kentucky, Joe and I ran together almost every day. They had moved to Sydney in 1983, about the time I left Lancaster with failing vision. It was great to see them again in Australia.

On one of my runs with Joe in Sydney, I noticed that my right foot was somewhat sore. I didn't remember twisting it or taking any missteps; it just hurt a bit. Two days later, I was back at home in Arizona. When I ran again, my foot hurt again. I thought at first that I may simply have been trying to run too much since I had been running twice daily on the beach in Adelaide. I took about three days off. To my surprise, my foot still hurt when I went out to run again on my familiar dirt trails in the Prescott National Forest. I concluded I may have sprained my foot while running on the sandy beach, even though I had been careful to keep my shoes on and not run barefoot. I decided to give myself a few more days of rest.

I continued this pattern of waiting a few more days and then trying again to run for a period of four weeks. Finally, in November 1992, I had an x-ray taken of my foot at the hospital. Everything looked normal on the x-ray.

Although I still tried to run every three or four days, my foot continued to hurt. In December I got a second x-ray, which still appeared normal. At this point, I figured I must have a stress fracture that just wasn't visible on plain x-rays. My running dropped off to a painful one-half to one mile once per week, when I would go out to see if it still hurt.

Repeat x-rays in March 1993 still were negative, but by then I had stopped running altogether. I was extremely frustrated. In twenty-eight years of running, I had never had an injury that kept me out of action for more than three weeks. I had been nursing this sore foot now for six months.

In May, I decided to spend the $640.00 to get a CAT scan of my foot. Finally, the fracture showed up. I had a fracture of the navicular bone in my right midfoot. I had already been seeing a podiatrist and had been outfitted with a rigid orthotic for my right foot. He recommended I get a second opinion about what I should do about this fracture. In the meantime, I strapped myself into a hard plastic cast boot held in place with Velcro® strips that I wore for thirteen weeks. In the cast, I could walk without foot pain. In my regular shoes, even with the orthotic, I had a painful limp.

I tried to be patient. I followed all of the doctor's suggestions. Neither of the two orthopedic surgeons I consulted recommended surgery. They felt it was better to wait and see if I could heal on my own. A second CAT scan in December 1993 again showed a non-healed fracture of the navicular bone. There was further separation of the fragments. The foot specialists all agreed that my running days were over.

That was terribly disheartening news. Even though I hadn't been able to walk without pain for nearly a year, I had still expected and hoped to get back to running. It had been my favorite recreation and exercise for twenty-eight years. It had also been the vehicle for most of my truly memorable and peak experiences. It had been my claim to fame. I was once the fastest insulin-dependent marathon runner in the country by my unofficial reckoning.

It had also been my identity. "I'm a long-distance runner," I'd always say to new people I would meet if they asked me what I liked to do. Now, I was faced with no longer being a runner. I remember telling Ellen about that second CAT scan report and then slipping into tears.

What else would I have to suffer? What else would I have to give up or let go of? Why did I keep getting hit with physical health problems or challenges? I fell deeply into a victim mindset, and I knew it was up to me to pull myself out of it.

One of the things I had always advised in my self-healing talks was to look for the lessons in every experience, even ones that feel like bad experiences such as this broken foot. In looking for the lessons, my first thought was that the foot injury forced me to slow down. I could no longer keep running in my life. I was forced to go at a slower pace. Perhaps I was simply trying to do too much, especially in my trip to Singapore and Australia. Maybe my foot was just telling me to slow down and get off my feet.

Over the weeks and months that followed, I started to recover from the initial grief over the loss of running and my identity crisis. With deeper reflection, I realized that I had been truly addicted to running. I had been using running as a mood-altering experience. It helped me escape from the stresses of my medical practice and the stresses of my recent speaking tour in Australia. As long ago as medical school, I had used running to escape the anxiety and pressure I felt from too much homework, too much to learn, and too little time to do it. Because I had worked closely with addicts in my medical practice, I recognized that I absolutely fit the mold.

Once I could label my running as an addiction, it was easier not to pine over losing it. I realized that my broken foot was an opportunity for me to break free of a very major addictive behavior in my life. It opened the door to learning more about my true feelings. It allowed me to experience my feelings more fully, rather than to dissipate them by running them off.

My approach to managing stress had to change. At the end of a stressful day at the office, my "stress fracture" would no longer allow me to go running in the woods to remove my stress. The irony was not lost on me.

Instead of going for a run, I reflected on what particular events or circumstances I was reacting to and how I could make things better. My life became fuller in many ways because I was more aware and accepting of my feelings.

Running had worked like an anesthetic for me. All the endorphins produced during a long run had numbed me to whatever feelings I had at the time, with the result that I wasn't able to fully process them.

Even though I could no longer go running, I became a healthier person emotionally. I certainly felt more alive and more appreciative of my life. Despite those insights, I still wished I could go out for a run at times. I still missed it.

With more reflections on addictions, I began to consider other addictions in my life and to work on them. My broken foot stopped more than my running.

More accurately, it was my broken feet, plural. My left foot had also fractured and collapsed. I knew that patients with diabetes with peripheral neuropathy in the foot and ankle could experience fractures and dislocations of bones and joints with minimal or no known trauma. Called Charcot arthropathy, this syndrome perfectly described what had happened to my feet.

I was no longer able to hike or ski or use my rollerblades or jump on our trampoline in our backyard. After two years off the slopes, I did successfully go downhill skiing in January 1995 without foot pain. I didn't expect to start running again. In the big picture, I was healthier without it.

17

What a Party!

If you bring forth what is within you, what you bring forth will save you. If you do not bring forth what is within you, what you do not bring forth will destroy you.
—The Gospel of Thomas, Verse 70, *Pagel's Gnostic Gospels*

Although I was no longer running or hiking due to my fractured feet, that didn't mean I was resigned to becoming a couch potato. I still wanted to challenge myself athletically and stay in shape. I had always enjoyed bicycling, which I could still do without foot pain, so I switched to bicycling as my main form of exercise.

We lived just two blocks from a great old railway bed that became my favorite riding trail. Typically, I would get out on the bike for about forty-five minutes in the evening after finishing work. The trail was well-graded, free of any old rail ties, and extended nearly thirty miles from my home, although I never rode the entire distance. The trail wound through the Prescott National Forest and provided a relatively smooth and scenic off-road experience. It made it possible for me to maintain my cardiovascular fitness, and I really grew to love my evening ramble on my bike.

When my Kentucky friends, Mark and Joni, told me about an amazing multi-day bicycle ride they had completed, I was immediately intrigued. In Alaska I had participated in a group bicycle ride from Anchorage to Homer, a distance of 250 miles in five days. What Mark and Joni described sounded like it would be even more fun, although more strenuous.

RAGBRAI XXII — 1994

The Register's Annual Great Bicycle Ride Across Iowa (RAGBRAI) takes place the last full week every July. First held in 1973, RAGBRAI is sponsored by the *Des Moines Register* and has become the bike-touring event with the most cyclists in the world. Mark and Joni had both completed this "Tour de Farms" several times and described it as a week-long party with the benefit of good exercise. They were both avid long-distance runners as well as bicyclists.

When I lived in Kentucky, they were my good running buddies as well as good friends, and Mark and I had both run the fifty-mile road race from Frankfurt to Louisville in 1980. I eagerly made plans to join them in Iowa for the next event, RAGBRAI XXII scheduled for July 24–30, 1994.

My Alaska bicycle ride from Anchorage to Homer, 250 miles in five days, was an incredible experience that made me eager to try the twice-as-long RAGBRAI bicycle ride in Iowa.

To prepare, I bicycled about one hour daily for the five months leading up to the event. On weekends, I would usually get in a two-hour ride at least one of the days. My longest training ride was thirty-five miles, which took me slightly over three hours in the mountains of my north central Arizona home.

The RAGBRAI ride moves from west to east and takes seven days to cross Iowa, a distance of about 500 miles. The small towns of Iowa bid for the opportunity to have the cyclists pass through their town, and that year six towns were chosen for overnight camping. Each year a different course is laid out with small country roads being chosen for the bicycle route and small towns for rest stops.

When it came time to fly to Omaha on July 23, 1994, I knew I could have been better trained. I was a little apprehensive about cycling seventy miles per day, but I figured I knew my body, and I could pace myself as slowly as needed. My primary objective was to have a good time and to enjoy being with my Kentucky friends. In addition to my friends Mark and Joni, Sherry was going to make the trek. Her husband, Colin, had been one of my partners in the medical practice in Lancaster, Kentucky from 1980 until 1983. I was looking forward to spending so much time together.

Even in 1994, RAGBRAI was a really big event. I was one of the 15,000 participants. In addition to all the cyclists, there were support team members, sponsors, single-day riders, and thousands of vendors. The vendors supplied Gatorade®, lemonade, beer, and water for the thirsty. They had pork chops and turkey drumsticks for the hungry, and a vast array of T-shirts, bicycle gear, and novelties for those inclined to shop.

I never saw so many bicycles or crazy bicycle riders in my life! I started meeting other RAGBRAI'ers as soon as I got off the plane in Omaha. Several of us all piled into a truck together to ride the thirty miles to Council Bluff, the official starting point.

A tent city was set up at the local fairgrounds. It was astonishing and magnificent. When I arrived there were bands playing, thousands of people and their bicycles, and a carnival atmosphere that continued the whole week.

When we set out on our bikes the next morning, there were so many bicyclists that one really had to be careful not to cause a bike wreck by swerving suddenly on the road. In the first hour, I stopped to help one cyclist who had crashed when another bike cut him off and hit his front wheel. Several people helped him off the road and out of harm's way. I later heard that he had been flown to Iowa City by helicopter with a broken hip.

I rode with Joni and Sherry that first morning. I knew I was pushing myself a bit to keep up with them, but I wasn't suffering. I really liked being on the small country roads, passing mile after mile of cornfields and pig farms. It reminded me so much of my childhood, growing up on the farm in Illinois. There were the same warm breezes, rank smells of the pig farms, and familiar rustling of growing corn.

I also had a great time stopping frequently at watermelon and lemonade stands. I was burning so many calories that I even had a big piece of homemade apple pie that first afternoon. It was a stellar day. I thoroughly enjoyed myself. When I finally set up my tent in the midst of the Kentucky contingent, I felt great. I was really glad I had decided to take on this adventure.

My day had gone well. I certainly felt a bit more tired. The next day, I decided to ride by myself rather than try to push myself to keep up with any of my friends. I met Joni, Mark, Sherry, and several others at lunch. The fresh hot corn-on-the-cob was incredible. We saw a man bicycling with a big blown-up plastic rocket strapped to his back. I also saw my first "bicycle built for three." I later found out there was even one "bicycle built for four" in the race. I thought that would be a great way to travel, and I wouldn't have to struggle to keep up with my buddies.

On the third day of cycling, I was really dragging. I felt sluggish and overtired. I had been going to bed early to give myself plenty of rest. Though I hadn't had any alcohol to drink, I definitely felt hungover.

I kept checking my blood sugar levels to make sure that wasn't the problem. My levels were fine. I also drank a lot of water to make sure I wasn't dehydrated. I was using one of the

Camelbak® water containers that are worn like a backpack. I drank a total of seven liters of water plus extra Gatorade® and lemonade, and also ate watermelon during that third day. I couldn't imagine that I was dehydrated, but I sure felt terrible.

When I finally got to the tent city that night, I felt nauseated and bloated. I wasn't at all hungry but decided to go along for the spaghetti dinner anyway. I knew I needed to refuel my body if I was going to keep up this amount of energy output. My friend Sherry, who was also a nurse, mentioned to me that my face and eyes looked puffy.

I was describing how poorly I felt to another Kentucky running friend, Dick, when it dawned on me what was wrong. I was not clearing my body's waste products. My kidneys weren't handling the stress of bicycling eight hours a day. I was going into some kind of kidney failure! It had been eight years since I had had any evidence of kidney failure, but here it was, staring me in my puffy face. I had visions of being transferred to the renal dialysis unit in Iowa City. It really scared me. When I went to bed that night, I had to fight back tears. The specter of kidney failure, dialysis, and ill health was too much for me to face.

The next morning, I arranged to ride in a car rather than on my bicycle, and to take the day off. I figured that if I gave myself twenty-four hours of rest, my kidneys might be able to clear out some of the toxins, and I could recover. My plan worked like a charm. I felt better and better as the day of rest unfolded. I rode in a Jeep with another cyclist who was suffering from an abscessed tooth. We drove together to Marshalltown, Iowa, the designated endpoint for day four. I walked around the town square and ate more sweet corn while he had his tooth pulled. When we parted ways that night to join our respective groups, we both felt better and planned to ride our bikes the next day.

While I was wandering around Marshalltown, resting and recovering, I called home to talk to my wife, Ellen. I wanted to share with her some of the feelings I was having. I had no idea how overwhelming that call would be. I got choked up before I could even tell her what had happened. As soon as I mentioned I thought it was my kidneys, I started crying. It was too hard to speak. The phone line was connected, but I couldn't talk. The flood of my emotions surprised me, and I think it worried Ellen also. She told me later that month that she had never experienced me feeling that bad.

Looking back at that day, I realize how upsetting it had been to face yet again my worst fear of a slow, sickly death from kidney failure. I thought I had overcome that nightmare in 1986. I had changed my diet, given up alcohol, started meditating, and changed my life dramatically to get better. But I still had some pretty significant fears to overcome and a lot to learn about myself.

I also realized that maintaining a stiff upper lip and not sharing my pain doesn't work for me. I made great gains that day in my willingness to be vulnerable by sharing my fear. I also got a big dose of homemade humble pie.

Growing up on the farm, I had learned firsthand about the old adage, "If you get kicked off the horse, you have to get right back on again." I recovered enough on my day off that I decided to ride my bike again on day five. I decided to get back onto my two-wheeled horse. I felt good riding all day and much better than I had on day three. I was delighted that my body was able to recover so quickly. I was still a bit shocked by how upset I had sounded on the phone with Ellen the night before.

On day six, I broke my camp at 6:00 a.m. I was dressed in my bike togs and had packed up my tent and sleeping bag by 6:20 a.m. I thought I was ready to roll by 6:30 a.m. with new air in my tires, and I expected to have another good day on my bike. When I carried my tent and spare gear across the schoolyard camp and loaded it on the truck, I felt exhausted. When I walked up the ramp to the back of the truck, I had to stop to rest. It suddenly dawned on me that I couldn't expect to ride seventy miles if I couldn't even carry my gear a short way across the schoolyard.

I decided I needed another day of rest. Taking care of my health was far more important than trying to keep up a good appearance or macho façade. Although I still worried a bit about what my friends might think, I decided that humility and health consciousness was what I most desired. So, I took a second day of rest.

The final day of RAGBRAI, day seven, was a great celebration. I was again feeling healthy. The end day of the ride was to Clinton, Iowa, and I took a shortcut rather than the regular bike route. My route was forty-four miles rather than the scheduled fifty-four miles.

I really enjoyed the solitude of riding alone, and I wanted to play it safe to make sure I would stay healthy. My plan worked well. In fact, I reached the broad expanse of the Mississippi River before any of my other friends. I even took time to stop for milk and cookies as I rode into Clinton. I was glad to be done with this particular adventure. I was relieved to be feeling fairly healthy. I was anxious to get the lab tests to find out what was going on with my kidneys.

As soon as I got home to Arizona, I applied myself to diagnosing and understanding what was happening to me. I noticed I was still puffy in the ankles and lower legs, symptoms consistent with retained fluid. My blood pressure was 160/90, which was quite high for me. This was concerning because elevated blood pressure contributes to decreased blood flow to the kidneys.

Two days after getting home, I attended a medical conference, "Renal Aspects of Hypertension." The final pieces of my medical puzzle fell into place.

From day one on the ride, I had been taking an anti-inflammatory medicine in an effort to minimize my aches and pains. The kidney expert at the conference pointed out that this particular medicine caused the most significant decrease in renal filtration. Furthermore, the level of exercise I had experienced could have raised my blood pressure. I had been bicycling both harder and longer than usual. All these factors—heavy exercise, elevated blood pressure, and the anti-inflammatory medicine—could have compromised my kidneys' ability to do their job.

After a week of rest, and no more anti-inflammatory medicines, my high blood pressure and ankle edema were gone. The 24-hour urine test for creatinine clearance showed I still had only slightly diminished kidney function. The nightmare about a renal dialysis unit in Iowa City evaporated. I went back to riding forty-five minutes daily, just to stay healthy. I knew that I would not stress my body with such a light load. I even occasionally increased my ride to two hours, checking my ankles for edema.

I certainly didn't plan to ride across Iowa again anytime soon, but what a party!

Golf

That fall I decided to take up an entirely new enterprise, just for the fun of it. I decided to play golf. As a long-distance runner, I had always pooh-poohed the game of golf. As I would run around the perimeter of a golf course, I would sometimes see golfers swinging those lightweight clubs and jumping into their golfcarts. I laughed to myself thinking that they considered that to be exercise. I never thought I'd ever be in their golf shoes.

There were a number of factors that led me to golf. With my foot broken and a non-union of the fracture, I was told by several doctors that I couldn't expect to run again. My wife had been telling me for months that I needed a hobby just to add balance to my life. I had heard that a new activity in mid-life could give us new enthusiasm, new meaning, new excitement, and rejuvenation. I had also been aware of the New Age teaching that picking an activity we considered to be strange and unlike ourselves could help open us up to parts of our personality that we may have been denying. Golf seemed to fit all those conditions for me.

I started playing on Wednesday afternoons in October 1994. Having only played golf about five times in my life, I played poorly at first. My initial golf partner was Tom, who was also the minister of the Unity Church of Prescott and my good friend. Tom was infinitely patient with me. He helped me pick the club to use and tried to help me develop a reasonable swing. It soon became obvious to me that I was going to like this game, so I started taking lessons. That really helped me improve my skills. Tom continued to play golf with me each week, and my game improved.

There were several interesting challenges in my game. From each tee, I couldn't see the green or the flag off in the distance. Therefore, I had to be pointed in the right direction and given some sort of target to aim at. Next, I couldn't see the ball once I hit it. My partner had to pay strict attention and then lead me to my ball. Finally, I always had to ride in a cart because my broken foot wouldn't allow me to walk the long distance of the course.

Despite the accommodations I had to make, I had a wonderful time learning and playing the game. In the six months after I started, my nine-hole score improved from 75 strokes to an average of 58 strokes. Golf turned into a great new hobby for me. What's more, after playing 18 holes, I actually felt that I'd gotten a lot of good exercise. It's a good thing I didn't mind all the egg on my face.

Healing Self and Others

My life as a family practitioner in Prescott was full of healing, being healed, and helping others with their healing. I kept busy with my medical practice, step-parenting, bicycling, golfing, driving my Mercedes, and being a husband.

Occasionally, I traveled to speak to groups of people with diabetes about self-healing. Occasionally I spoke to doctors about how to help their patients live well with diabetes.

Eventually, my kidneys began to fail, and I couldn't stop the failing. By 2007, people with type 1 diabetes could qualify for either kidney dialysis or kidney transplant. It had been twenty-two years since I first experienced kidney failure in 1985. That's a lot longer time than the eighteen months until failure that I had first been made aware of. I also was advised that I could get both a kidney and a pancreas transplant at the same time.

My diabetes, which had been paramount in shaping my life, was finally eradicated on September 15, 2007, with a kidney/pancreas transplant. I was the 92nd Mayo Clinic patient and the 27th at the Scottsdale, Arizona facility to have this life-changing surgery. After forty-three years of living with type 1 diabetes, I was no longer a diabetic! I considered it a medical miracle.

In 2008, finally free of diabetes, I was still practicing family medicine, giving seminars, and thoroughly enjoying my life.

Of course, I was still visually impaired, and the injuries to my feet continued to prevent hiking and running.

I closed my practice and fully retired on May 1, 2020. Two months later I turned seventy years old. I had practiced medicine for forty-four years.

I came to realize that healing is a lifelong process, and I recognized that there was still a lot of self-healing for me to do. Retirement gave me the time to explore my faith in a deeper way, travel for relaxation instead of work, and take advantage of new medical advances as my body continued to reflect the ravages of a disease I'd lived with since I was fourteen.

All in all, I have been very happy and thankful for the fullness of my life. I have had countless blessings, sometimes disguised as hardships.

I am committed to continuing my personal growth and spiritual expansion. I continue to take classes and courses to learn more about the various modalities of healing. My self-healing continues and is accelerating. My favorite affirmations currently are:

"I have fabulous intuition and glorious guidance."

"I am radiant, joy-filled and magnificent."

"I am at peace."

APPENDIX

Factors in Healing

As I traveled and spoke about healing, I met many people who were struggling with their own illnesses and who were looking to me for hope. I was happy to offer hope. I believed there was always good reason for hope, not just because resignation is deadly, but because I have seen that life is so full of possibilities.

During my own periods of recurring blindness and recovery, I would reflect on my efforts to heal, and I'd wonder if the visualizations and affirmations, the running, and participation in positive emotional experiences, plus everything else I was doing were really making a difference. Would they have made a difference without my vitrectomy surgery? Would my body have healed without any help at all?

The fact that I regained my sight did not prove the methods I was using were effective. But scientific evidence supporting these methods has built steadily over the years.

The Role of Traditional Medicine in Healing

Through modern medicine, we can often work miracles. We can also fail miserably, and often this is because we neglected to involve the patient. In an effort to be efficient, we've trained people to give up their own power to the expert. In my own practice, I would often discuss with people the pros and cons of different options and ask their opinion.

Sometimes people would say, "Well, you tell me. You're the doctor."

My response to that would be, "Well, it's not my health problem, it's your health problem. But I will give you my recommendations if you want."

Peter Lee Powers, M.D.

I expected people who came to me to ask questions and get involved. I also learned that not every sick person who sought my professional opinion wanted to be healed. If the person would tell me what he/she wanted from me, we could often get to the heart of the matter more quickly. We all need to get more into the habit of asking for what we want.

It sometimes surprised my patients that I wouldn't take responsibility for their healing. In my opinion, a doctor is a consultant. And a person needs to get a health consultant he/she trusts and relates to. If a doctor isn't willing to listen to a client's point of view or discuss treatment, it may be time to find a new doctor.

Exercise

When I spoke to diabetic groups around the country, I often asked how many in the group were following a regular exercise program. I found that those who exercised regularly were generally in the minority, even though the benefits of exercise on both the mind and the body have been well demonstrated and publicized. Of special interest to diabetics is a study that showed that runners who did ten miles a day had lower than normal blood insulin levels. Exercise lowers insulin requirements, but perhaps even more significantly, it makes the available insulin more effective.

At one presentation, a man in the audience raised his hand and said, "I'm just so tired at the end of the day that I don't have the energy to exercise." I asked what kind of work he did that was so tiring. "I dig postholes all day long," he replied. I assured him that digging postholes qualified as exercise.

Perhaps there is an aversion to exercise because we've learned to think that it's only good for us if we don't enjoy it. The best exercise for you is the kind you most enjoy, whether it's walking, surfing, hoeing the garden, or playing hide-and-seek with your kids.

Nutrition

The American Diabetes Association (ADA), the American Cancer Society (ACS), and the American Heart Association (AHA), all recommend essentially the same diet. Anyone who wants to enjoy better health would do well to follow their guidelines for a healthy diet that emphasizes vegetables, fruits, whole grains, lean meats, and fish. Specifically, the ACS and AHA recommend less saturated fat, salt, and sugar, and more fiber and roughage.

The ADA guideline for nutrition therapy recommends eating a variety of healthy foods in appropriate portion sizes. The guideline suggests that you should choose an eating plan (Mediterranean diet, DASH diet, vegetarian, or low-carb) that works best for your personal food preferences and lifestyle.

A visit to a dietician can be extremely helpful in setting up a dietary program to fit individual needs.

In my own healing process, I made two dietary changes that made a noticeable difference. Wanting to do everything possible to help my body, I stopped drinking alcohol. Subsequently, I felt sharper, and more alert and energetic than I had previously. Later, when my kidneys began to fail, I discovered that an excess of protein in my diet had been making me feel slow and weak. By cutting my protein intake, I regained so much energy that I was able to start running marathons again after a seven-year layoff.

Keeping Open to the Possibilities

The diagnosis of diabetes was an early death sentence prior to the 20th century. The discovery of insulin in 1921 was nothing short of miraculous for people with diabetes. Glucose monitoring, which became widely available in 1981 only a year after it came onto the market, is often considered the second most momentous development in the history of diabetes. It provided diabetics with a timely, accurate, inexpensive way to monitor blood sugar levels.

Discoveries and technological advancements continue to offer many possibilities for greater health. However, there are other healing pathways worth exploring. Examples discussed below include visualization and affirmations.

Visualization and Healing

The power of the mind to heal the body is a realm that we have only begun to recognize and use. Carl Simonton, M.D., and his wife, Stephanie, were pioneers in the use of visualization to treat cancer and have offered striking anecdotal and statistical evidence for the value of visualization in healing. In their 1978 bestselling classic, *Getting Well Again*, they reported a survival rate of twice the national norm (over a four-year period) among 159 cancer patients who used visualization in conjunction with traditional cancer therapies. A full 15 percent of these patients whose cancer had been diagnosed as incurable had their cancer go into remission or disappear.

In the years since then, the mind-body connection has been well-established, and cancer centers around the country provide patients with information on visualization techniques such as guided meditation and guided imagery to reduce stress and visualize healing. The Simonton Cancer Center, a nonprofit wellness organization, offers virtual online programs and retreats.

1. O. Carl Simonton, Stephanie Matthews-Simonton, James L. Creighton, Getting Well Again (J. P. Tarcher, 1978).

Affirmations, Shedding Hurtful Baggage

What we say to ourselves is the most powerful force in our lives. Our beliefs create our experience. By simply starting to notice the negative thoughts we have about ourselves and then gently turning negatives into positives, we can begin to change our experience.

Some affirmations that I have used are:
"I am taking better control of my diabetes and my life."
"I like myself."
"I am vital and energized."
"I am whole and complete."

"I am safe."
"I am seeing better and better."
"My vision is continuing to improve."
"I am good at controlling my blood sugar."
"I am eating well."
"I accept myself exactly the way I am."
"I am healthy and actively exercising."

"I am an open, gentle, joyful, powerful human being unconditionally healing myself and you with my love."

An Attitude of Personal Responsibility

In *The Complete Guide to Your Emotions and Your Health*, Emrika Padus and the editors of *Prevention Magazine* reported an interesting attitude study of breast cancer patients in England:

"[R]esearchers classified the women according to the way they responded to the diagnosis of breast cancer. They found four distinct approaches to the disease among the women they interviewed.

"Some women reacted with complete denial that any of the signs of their disease were serious. The denial was so complete that some patients told the researchers after mastectomies that their breasts had been removed only 'as a precaution.' Other women took the attitude that they could personally fight and defeat the disease. They tried to find out everything they could about breast cancer in order to conquer it. A third group acknowledged that they had cancer, accepted the diagnosis stoically, and made no effort to find out anything more about the disease. The last group reacted by simply giving up. They felt totally powerless to improve their conditions and resigned themselves to an early death.

"There were dramatic differences in the survival rates of the four groups. Of the patients who responded to their diagnosis with either denial of the existence of the disease or a firm fighting spirit, 75 percent were alive and well five years later. Only 35 percent of the other women, those who either accepted their fate stoically or gave up completely, were still alive at that time. (Greer, Morris, and Pettingale 1979)."

In regard to my own healing, I was certainly in a denial stance. "I refuse to be blind" was an important factor in my recovery to being able to see again in one eye.

In a later study published in 2005 that tracked more than 500 women for up to ten years who had been diagnosed with early stage (I and II) breast cancer, the women who had a helpless or hopeless response to their initial diagnosis were more likely to relapse or die (Watson, Homewood, Haviland, and Bliss 2005).

Bernie Siegel, the widely known author of *Love, Medicine and Miracles*, has worked extensively with cancer support groups. He has said, "Hope acts as a placebo. And there is no question that placebos can affect the immune system."

2. Emrika Padus and Prevention Magazine editors. *The Complete Guide to Your Emotions and Your Health* (Rodale Press, 1986).
3. S. Greer, T. Morris, and K. W. Pettingale. "Psychological Response to Breast Cancer: Effect on Outcome," *Lancet 314*, no. 8146, (1979):785-787.
4. M. Watson, Janis Homewood, Jo Haviland, and Judith M. Bliss, "Influence of psychological response on breast cancer survival: 10-year follow-up of a population-based cohort," *European Journal of Cancer 41* (2005):1710-1714.
5. Bernie S. Siegel, *Love, Medicine & Miracles: Lessons Learned About Self-Healing from a Surgeon's Experience with Exceptional Patients* (Harper & Row, Publishers, Inc., 1986).

Not Being Responsible for Others

At a seminar in Seattle, my wife, Ellen, participated in some group discussions with spouses of other diabetics. Many of these spouses expressed frustration at trying to help manage the diabetes of their partners. They talked about having to call ambulances to rescue their spouses, or having to feed them when they got so hypoglycemic that they couldn't feed themselves, or having to check their blood sugar or give them their insulin. Taking responsibility for other people tends to create a circular, destructive pattern commonly known as codependency.

This kind of caretaking was all foreign to Ellen because she had never done any of this for me. She pointed out to the group that it was not their responsibility to be looking after their partners' diabetes.

Later, when it was my turn to speak, I encouraged the spouses to detach themselves from that caretaking frustration. This is another one of those cases where "helping" can really hurt.

I had always cringed when I saw parents administering an older child's insulin or constantly telling a child what he or she should or shouldn't eat. This type of helping gives a message of disempowerment. A healthier message is that we are each responsible for and powerful over our own lives and no one else's.

When I went blind from diabetes, my family felt this loss very acutely. Their distress about my blindness was so great that I felt like I was carrying an extra burden in worrying about how they were handling my illness. Worrying about my family's reaction was so stressful that later, when my kidneys began to deteriorate, I kept the news entirely to myself. I didn't want to feel responsible for anyone's distress over my illness. It would have been healthier for me to have seen my family's distress as their own choice and responsibility, not mine. It would have freed up a lot of healing energy for both of us to break this destructive cycle of worrying about each other.

Taking Personal Responsibility Doesn't Mean Feeling Guilty

I believe everyone makes mistakes. We have the opportunity to learn something every time we make a mistake. Sometimes, a mistake allows us to learn something we couldn't have learned any other way. As long as we learn from our mistakes, they are not bad. We certainly don't want to punish ourselves for them. If we feel ashamed or guilty, or self-critical, it is a reminder for us to be more self-accepting. It calls us to a greater self-love. If we can grow into greater self-love and self-acceptance, the mistake has turned into something helpful for us, which is a good thing.

Friendship

The support and love of friends is another factor that I believe helps create an emotional environment for healing. In *The Roseto Story: An Anatomy of Health*, authors John G. Bruhn and Stewart Wolf, M.D. tell about Roseto, a small Italian-American community in Pennsylvania that in the 1960s had one of the nation's lowest incidences of fatal heart disease. This statistic puzzled researchers because Rosetans were not unusual in their smoking, exercising, or eating habits. Studying Roseto more closely, researchers found that Roseto's most significant difference from other communities was that it was a tight knit community, bound by strong ties of kinship and friendship.

According to Dr. Wolf, "There was a remarkable cohesiveness and sense of unconditional support within the community. Family ties were very strong. . . No one was ever abandoned." During the late 60s, as children grew up and moved away, the values of the community began to change, and the town's incidence of fatal heart disease rose until it was on par with other nearby communities.

Based on volumes of carefully gathered evidence, Dr. Wolf concluded that the Roseto story "clearly demonstrates that the most important factors in health are the intangibles—things like trust, honesty, loyalty, team spirit. In terms of preventing heart disease, it's just possible that morale is more important than jogging or not eating butter."

In my own experience, friendships have been important, not only in terms of shared love and support, but also for the opportunity to play, laugh, communicate, and express emotions. When I was ill, these things helped me feel joy and the will to live. They mobilized my healing energies.

6. John G. Bruhn and Stewart Wolf, *The Roseto Story: An Anatomy of Health* (Norman: University of Oklahoma Press, 1979).

Seeing Obstacles as Opportunities, Rediscovering Love

I believe that we are beings of love by our very nature. This love gets covered up from the time of infancy by layers of hurt and socialization. We never lose the yearning for love, which we know from somewhere but seem to have lost. Along our paths we rediscover love by letting go of the things that cover it up. Our efforts at living, healing, and dying can be viewed most profoundly in the context of this love.

The deepest hurts are only temporary, and they can be healed in an atmosphere of love. One can see hurt and pain as the bringing to awareness of something that is ready to be healed. Seen in this way, hurts and illnesses can be an opportunity to grow in love, awareness, and happiness.

Obstacles can be seen as opportunities. Because I lived with diabetes, I was a much better doctor. Because I'd been a patient, I could be a much more compassionate physician. Because I'd seen death and how fragile life is, I could better appreciate the miracle of each day and each moment. Perhaps the greatest gift my diabetes gave me is that through it I rediscovered my love for myself and acceptance of myself. This was a wonderful discovery.

Expressing Emotions

One significant step in the healing process is to begin to express our emotions. I saw patients almost every day in my practice who were experiencing symptoms of illness that decreased and often disappeared completely as soon as some of their suppressed or deeply held feelings could be expressed.

I believe every individual has the ability to experience self-healing by increasing his or her awareness of their feelings, their beliefs, and their negative thoughts, and then changing some or all of them.

I often asked my patients to try to identify what possible decision they might have made about life or about themselves when some dramatic or traumatic event happened in their life. Even if that decision was made twenty, thirty, or sixty years earlier, it often can still be having a profound effect on a person's life.

I became aware that I had come to believe that I would die young due to my diabetes. I really don't know when I came to believe that. It may have started when I first was diagnosed with diabetes, and I was told about all the life-threatening complications of the illness. It may have been a gradual decision after seeing so many young people with diabetes die while I was in training to become a doctor of family medicine.

In any case, I have learned that such a negative belief as "I will die young from diabetes" had a profoundly negative effect on my life that I struggled to overcome. For example, I would be tempted to ask why should I bother to go to the trouble of following a special diet or to avoid good desserts or to prick my finger with those painful lancets if I was going to die young anyway?

If the negative thoughts are rampant enough, the effect can be even more devastating. If I held the belief that not only would I die young but that my life held nothing but pain and suffering and sickness, I might have just given up. Not only might I not have bothered to take good care of myself because of feeling hopeless, but I might have stopped bothering to look both ways when I crossed the street.

A dramatic example of the power of our emotions and the value in expressing them occurred with a patient of mine who had asthma. She was in her mid-fifties and had raised twelve children when I first met her. When I asked her about her childhood, she had shared with me that it had been very abusive. Her parents had been poor, and her stepfather had physically abused her up until the age of thirteen when she had left home.

It is well recognized in the medical field that asthma is a condition directly affected by psychological factors. Often, people with asthma have a worse time breathing when they are under a lot of stress.

My patient came to the emergency room one day with severe bronchial spasm and respiratory distress. She was unable to get enough oxygen into her lungs because of the bronchial spasm, and she was suffocating.

I treated her with oxygen and intravenous medications to reverse the bronchospasms and had used three or four different medicines and repeated breathing treatments in the emergency room, but she was still not improving. The only intervention that remained was to paralyze her breathing muscles and put her on a respirator. This would provide mechanical ventilation.

Before taking that drastic step, I decided to have a "heart-to-heart" talk with her. I wanted to see if I could uncover any psychological factors that might be making matters worse. I asked her if anything was upsetting her other than the trouble she was having with breathing.

She said no.

I asked her if anyone had upset her or if anything had upset her a lot in the last few days.

Again, she said no.

Finally, I asked her if there was any important anniversary around this time of year or if anything had happened to her in the long ago past at this time of year.

She said she didn't think so. She sat on the edge of the bed in the emergency room, gasping for breath with IV fluids and medicines and oxygen running, still pondering my question. She could barely talk.

Suddenly, lights of recognition came on in her eyes. She told me that this was the exact time of year when she was sold by her parents.

Incredulous, I asked her to explain what had happened.

I learned that at age thirteen, she had been sold by her stepfather to help raise a little money for her family to buy food for the younger sisters and brothers. She was sold to a man who kept her as a slave and sex object from age thirteen to twenty-one. She said she was often chained to a post when he would be away from the house all day long just so she wouldn't run away. She said some days he would lock her into a dark room all day without food, and she would have to use one corner of her room for a toilet.

After seven years of living like this, she ran away on the day after her twenty-first birthday. She had realized that once she had turned twenty-one years old, no one could make her go back to that man. She knew that if she got arrested, the police wouldn't make her go back.

As we talked about this horrible experience, her breathing started to get better. Her words seemed to come easier once she really started talking about her feelings. It was apparent to me that there was still a huge amount of pent-up anger and resentment in her. She had been living with this pain for more than forty years.

The man who had abused her and her stepfather who had sold her had both been dead for many years, but the hurting was still doing its damage. I advised her to write each of these men a letter. We agreed she would be in the hospital for a few days until her breathing was better. She agreed to write a letter to each of these men. I encouraged her to express all the feelings she had held inside.

On the next day she had finished both of these letters, which I refer to as "completion letters." I had her tear the letters into small pieces and throw them away. Then I had her go to work on writing a letter to her mother, who was still living. I wanted her to express the feelings to her mother, who had gone along with the plan and allowed her to be sold at age thirteen.

This letter was not intended to be sent to her mother, who was in her late seventies and frail. It was only an exercise to help express her feelings. It took two days and a lot of encouragement for her to write this letter.

After writing to her mother about how angry and hurt she had felt all her life, she definitely started to feel better. We destroyed that letter also. Her breathing continued to improve.

On the final hospital day, she decided to write another letter to her mother to talk about those terrible things that had happened to her. She had never talked about any of this with her mother in all these forty years. At the end of this letter, she told me she realized how abused and beaten her own mother was, and she had decided to write to her mother that she forgave her for letting her stepfather sell her. This letter, she did mail to her mother.

By the time she was discharged from the hospital, her breathing was dramatically improved, and some of her long-held hurts had been released. When she came back to see me in the office a week later, she had been able to cut back on her breathing medicine to about half as much as she had needed when she had left the hospital.

In this particular case, just writing a few letters helped to unleash this woman's deeply held feelings. Sometimes it takes writing a letter to a person over and over again to find some of the more deeply buried feelings. I often encouraged patients to express their feelings in one of these completion letters by rewriting the letter many times.

The process can still be valuable as long as there is any anger, blame, or resentment being expressed. A good test of whether one is finished with this completion letter process is if one would be willing to receive this letter from someone else. That is, does this version of the letter contain only love, understanding, and forgiveness? I recommend that only this final letter be sent to the person who may have caused the hurt so long ago. The value in this exercise is in being able to express all the feelings.

Made in the USA
Middletown, DE
18 February 2025

71059908R00116